Answers from the World's
Leading Authority on
Asperger's Syndrome /
High-Functioning Autism

Craig R. Evans with Dr. Tony Attwood

Advance Praise for *Ask Dr. Tony*

"Who in the autism community has ever wished for a direct line to Dr. Tony At-twood? Or has spent time wondering what Dr. Attwood would think about the problems and situations that frustrate our lives as people with autism? This book is full of thoughtfully crafted questions originally asked by the autism community and answered through discussion between Dr. Attwood and C. Evans with care and concern. It is a gift."

> — Lisa Morgan, author of *Living Through Suicide Loss with
> an Autism Spectrum Disorder – An Insider Guide for
> Individuals, Family, Friends, and Professional Responders*

"Absolutely smashing! Dr. Tony Attwood's advice is world-class. He completely understands the ASD mind and covers a wide range of much-needed advice for everyday life. As one of the Aspie mentors in *Been There. Done That. Try This!*, I highly recommend this book to those on the autism spectrum as well as parents and all involved with autism. Tony and Craig have knocked it out of the park!"

> — Anita Lesko, BSN, RN, MS, CRNA, autism activist, United
> Nations guest speaker, author of *Temple Grandin: The
> Stories I Tell My Friends* and *The Complete Guide to Autism
> and Healthcare*

"This collection of interviews between Dr. Tony Attwood, who steadfastly remains the most revered expert in Asperger's syndrome, and the insightful and positive author Craig Evans is wonderful! It's an easy read that delivers difficult concepts eloquently and respectfully."

> — Liane Holliday Willey, EdD, author of *Pretending to be
> Normal and Safety Skills for Asperger Women*

Advance Praise for *Ask Dr. Tony*

"Distilled from years of discussion on the "Ask Dr. Tony" show, Craig and Tony gift the autism community with easy-to-understand explanations combined with practical solutions for addressing some of the most vexing challenges facing individuals on the autism spectrum. This book is a must-read for anyone seeking greater appreciation of ASD individuals as an expression of the diversity of the human gene pool. In summary, the best of Dr. Tony Attwood brought to you by Craig Evans!"

> — Stephen Mark Shore, EdD, internationally known educator,
> author, and presenter on topics related to autism

"Over twenty-five years ago, a fragile mother of two wrote three letters to Dr. Tony, praying for a moment of his time during his visit and to get the answer to the question, 'Could I have autism?' He pulled her out of the line, sat her down on the back of the stage, and gently gave her the answer. This book is that moment given repeatedly, answering many people's pressing questions. With Craig Evans, Tony Attwood addresses the questions you've been needing answered the same way—kindly, gently, and with patience."

> — Dena L. Gassner, MSW, adjunct professor, PhD candidate
> Adelphi University, national board member Arc US, training
> consultant: NYU NEST, facilitator: AHANY

"There's a reason I watch videos with the captions turned on: catching the nuance of tone, the challenge of perspective, the speed of banter, and the import of content all at once is like isolating notes in a score the very first time the music plays. Which is why this book is so ingenious. Craig Evans has repackaged the fleeting flurry of video, transcribing and regifting Dr. Attwood's insight and heart so that audiences can engineer their own learning pace and style. Plainly written and alive with conversation, it's a great resource for empowering engagement, spurring independent thinking, and supporting active incorporation."

> — Jennifer Cook O'Toole, author of the *Asperkids* series,
> *Autism in Heels*, and contributing author to *Been There.*
> *Done That. Try This!*

ASK DR. TONY

Answers from the World's Leading Authority on Asperger's Syndrome / High-Functioning Autism

All marketing and publishing rights guaranteed to and reserved by:

FUTURE HORIZONS INC.

721 W. Abram Street
Arlington, TX 76013
(800) 489-0727
(817) 277-0727
(817) 277-2270 (fax)
E-mail: info@fhautism.com
www.fhautism.com

ISBN: 9781941765807

Contents

Ask Dr. Tony

How This Book
Came About

About the "Ask Dr. Tony" Question and Answer Program

How This Book Came About

"Never believe that a few caring people can't change the world.
For, indeed, that's all who ever have." — *Margaret Mead*

My name is Craig Evans. In 2006, I started Autism Hangout: a website dedicated to bringing positive, hopeful messages about autism to the world. It seemed the right thing to do, as most of what was online at that time was dreadfully discouraging. Besides, there was a deep, personal interest in my quest: I was trying to understand my future stepchild with Asperger's. To say I was fascinated with the gifts and shocked with the constraints of autism was an understatement. Autism Hangout was to be my portal to find answers and encouragement... and bring them to the autism community.

www.autismhangout.com

I sought out autism thought-leaders—authors, medical profession-als and researchers, speakers, therapists and counselors, teachers, social workers, community/public servants, and people living suc-cessfully with ASD—from around the globe and invited them to par-ticipate in a short, videotaped online interview where they could share their current thinking on successfully living with autism. The idea was to find what's happening now and bring this knowledge and advice to the public. If you've been touched by autism, you quickly recognize there are not many available answers, and there is no time to waste. As a media venue, Autism Hangout could make a difference in the lives of many. So, I immediately became a field reporter.

Many of those I interviewed touched me with their dedication, passion, enthusiasm, and pos-itive attitudes. Among them are the late Donna Williams, Dr. Stephen Shore, and Anita Lesko: all people with Asperger's living full, exciting lives with thriving careers. As "Aspie mentors," their wisdom combined with over twenty oth-er Aspie elders contributed to the 2013 seminal book *Been There. Done That. Try This!*

The concept of an "Aspie mentor" was first discussed in an online interview I'd recorded with a noted autism researcher, practitioner, author, and speaker from Brisbane, Australia named Dr. Tony Att-wood. He was so encouraging and engaging. His contagious enthusi-asm for the gifts of autism and how they could be harnessed to ben-efit humanity was remarkable. Doctor Tony was light-years ahead of all of us in his positive approach to autism. It gave me an idea.

I approached Dr. Attwood with the idea of an ongoing question and answer video program to bring his knowledge and enthusiasm to the autism community. "Yes! Yes! Let's do this!" he answered. "There are so many good questions and not enough available an-swers. Books take time and people can't often attend conferences.

How This Book Came About

If we can get answers to issues that help people now, let's do that!" So, in January of 2009, we launched the Ask Dr. Tony show.

The mechanics of producing the program were quite simple. I asked the 2,500 members of Autism Hangout to submit questions. Thanks to the growing list of Autism Hangout video reports online, we started to receive questions from those viewers, as well. Since Dr. Tony lives fifteen hours away in Brisbane, Australia, we had to set aside time well in advance to record via video chat. From there, I edited the conversations into over forty shows that remain online.

By 2014, due to time constraints and costs, I reluctantly shut down Autism Hangout. I'd filmed close to 300 interviews, now saved for

"Ask Dr. Tony - Answers!"

Living with Autism
Addiction to Drugs. What Can a Parent Do?

posterity at the Autism Hangout channel on the web, and they've been watched! Some have topped 50,000 views and a few are approaching 100,000 views. However, if just one person has been helped by these recordings, Dr. Tony and I both agree it was worth all the effort.

In October of 2016, Dr. Tony came to Minneapolis for a presentation. He asked to meet with me. Shortly after I closed Autism Hangout, he'd written asking me to consider keeping the Ask Dr. Tony program going. "People still need immediate information. I would like to continue the Ask Dr. Tony show when you're ready!" What could I say? So, in September 2017, Dr. Tony and I restarted the program.

During an Ask Dr. Tony taping in December 2017, we started to discuss the value of the previously answered questions in the Autism Hangout archive. The thought of converting those conversations into a book was discussed and decided on the spot; "We're doing it!" A few short months later, thanks to the fine folks at Future Horizons, you're now holding it.

Today people browse and consume information through the web (videos, music, news), but it quickly passes from public attention and seems to be just as quickly forgotten. Books stand the test of time. Besides, refreshing Dr. T's thoughts for new audiences seemed to be an ideal way of keeping helpful information present and available to the public. So, with this first book we're both hoping to reintroduce helpful, relevant knowledge from these past programs to those loving and living with autism.

If you've got a question about autism, please leave it at www.autismhangout.com. Hopefully, we'll be answering it and others for many years to come!

Our goal: Thriving with autism!

— *Craig R. Evans*
www.autismhangout.com

Introduction

The following is a transcript of a 2010 program about Dr. Tony Attwood. It not only tells you about this extraordinary human being, but it also serves as a primer for how this book works!

Introduction

"Ten Minutes with Dr. Tony."

CRAIG: Hello again everybody. This is Craig Evans of Autism Hangout, thank you for tuning into this Autism Hangout special report. I had a rare opportunity today to meet one of my heroes in autism, Dr. Tony Attwood, at a conference in Wisconsin that was sponsored by the AEP connections company. He's been pressed all day, but generously took a few moments with me to answer some questions. Dr. Tony, I just listened to a day of encouragement and enlightenment.

DR. TONY: Thank you.

CRAIG: I wanted to tell you this firsthand, because as a parent of a child with Asperger's syndrome it's very easy to get discouraged. When I was watching you today and hearing the depth of your knowledge, I was not only inspired, I was encouraged. Your attitude of hopefulness toward what these kids can be is nothing so short of exemplary. I wanted to be able to tell you that in person.

DR. TONY: Thank you. I take that to my heart.

CRAIG: I have come to know you mostly through the Ask Dr. Tony series, where we've had one-on-one conversations. I'm also familiar with your book. But one thing I know about you for sure is you genuinely, genuinely, care about these precious people. I find that inspirational, but how did you come about this lifelong passion to help this population?

DR. TONY: Fantastic question, one that I've been thinking about for some time. I'm going to give you a complex answer. It first began when I was nineteen. I went as a volunteer at a special school. I met two children with severe autism in 1971. I knew a bit about child development because I'd been studying psychology since I was fourteen; I always knew I wanted to be a psychologist. I'd studied social psychology. I also had a sister who was only three years old, so I knew a bit about early childhood development as well. These kids challenged all the established theories of child development—not only an intellectual level, but also at a compassionate level. The things that were upsetting to the kids were so interesting. Russell had a splinter in his finger, and he objected not to the splinter, but to me holding his finger to pull the splinter out. When he was upset, affection and consoling didn't work. He would spend hours just rolling around, and around, and around, or playing with water. I was fascinated. I thought, "That's it. I'm going to make a career of understanding such kids." I would love to go back to see those two children, Sarah and Russell, who switched me on to ASD. They must now be in their late thirties or forties.

The next question you might have is, how did I know? When I look at people, and meet people who work in the area, what's very common is that they have a relative with these characteristics.

They're what I call "bilingual." They understand the culture from an early age. My stepfather, who my mother married when I was six years old, is an engineer and hasn't been formally diagnosed. I remember as a child of six being fascinated by his differences; that there was this person who came into my life. I thought, "What planet does he come from? This is amazing!" I also watched how my mother changed to accommodate his personality and abilities.

Introduction

I think from very early on, there was that component. I also think that when you look at genetics, you will have people with Asperger's in a family history. Who do people with Asperger's marry? Extreme neurotypicals, and dotted with in the same family will be extreme neurotypicals.

It's extreme neurotypicals who understand Aspie. I think that in the family genetics—possibly on my side of a family, too—there may be a history of Asperger's. That means that they've got a lot of extreme neurotypicals. When we find a kid with Asperger's, there's a higher

risk of brothers and sisters being Aspie. Also, a higher "risk," if you call it that, of my brothers and sisters being extreme neurotypicals. I think that's one of the factors.

CRAIG: It's being bilingual.

DR. TONY: Bilingual. Yes, understanding the culture. It's not strange, you know. You read the signals. You know how to calm the person down. You know how to speak their language. You know how to be direct. You can understand the special interests. It's not weird ("What on Earth are you doing?"), it's sort of a feeling of, "I know this. I feel familiar with it."

CRAIG: One of the other adjectives I learned in hearing your talk is that you are so hopeful. Hope is very important when you have a child on the spectrum. In your opinion, what is most hopeful aspect of autism today?

DR. TONY: I've been here long enough to see successes: my sister-in-law, Penny, would probably have been put in an institution but for parental support. When we look at successful outcomes, it's usually a mixture of the parents being accepting of the person, encouraging them, and knowing when to support. Also, very important is knowing when to back off, to let the person learn. The personality of the individual concerned is important, too. Some decide, "Okay, I'm not going to blame others. I'm not going blame myself. I'm going to do something about it." There's something about that internal personality.

They may come across, in their lives, people who have given them advice and support and held their hand along the road. They may have met people who have not been good to them, but have sufficient balance of good people that have supported them. Also, the successful outcome in part has been by a successful career, which I think is very important. A network of support within the family, a support group in terms of friends or colleagues, and a sense of enjoyment of the special interests are a counterbalance to the adversity of life. All contribute to an effective means of managing one's emotions.

We've all seen examples of extreme emotions. If you can conquer those, life is a lot easier. I have seen successful outcomes of my clinical experience and current research which suggests that about 15 percent of those with Asperger's, over time, move into the subclinical normal range. They're eccentric. They're what I call very British. I have family members and friends and colleagues with Asperger's syndrome. I don't see it as a disaster, I see it as someone who is different and is embracing difference.

CRAIG: A successful life may not necessarily mean the neurotypical model of just family and children. It might just be satisfaction with who you are, and the job that you've chosen.

DR. TONY: Absolutely. I think one of the best examples is Temple Grandin.

CRAIG: Yes.

DR. TONY: She is very happy and sees herself defined by what she does rather than her relationship circle. Her satisfaction is the cattle industry and supporting people with autism. Altruistically, she's helped thousands of people throughout the world with her knowledge. There's a sense of self-worth, and that's what the person is looking for: self-worth. It can be identified in many ways, and I say, "What is Asperger's? Asperger's syndrome is someone who has found something more interesting than socializing."

CRAIG: For the folks at Autism Hangout, if you have stories of success of your loved one with Asperger's or ASD, please write it in. We need to document more of these stories, such as Temple's success. We all know that they're out there. The last question is, what three messages do you want to share most with the world about autism?

DR. TONY: Understand it, use it, and love it.

CRAIG: Understand it, use it, and love it.

DR. TONY: Yes.

CRAIG: Maybe we can pick up this on another time, when you've rested a bit, because that is wonderful. I love it.

DR. TONY: Okay. Thanks, Craig. [laughs] Good questions!

Ask Dr. Tony

Book Structure

Book Structure

The contents of this book are organized according to the results of a 2012 proprietary research study conducted for the book *Been There. Done That. Try This! The 17 Ranked Issues That Cause the Most Stress to Someone with Asperger's/ HFA*. The Emotional Availability category was combined with Intimacy, Dating, Sex, and Marriage as the submitted Ask Dr. Tony questions overlapped. The final chapter, Living with Autism, is a grouping of questions that did not fit into any particular category.

Bonus Sections "Questions and Answers from Global Autism Conferences" and "Answers to the Most Common Questions about Autism" are at the end of the book.

As this book has been designed to be read by sections, you may notice some repeated questions as they are pertinent in different chapters.

THE 17 RANKED ISSUES THAT CAUSE THE MOST STRESS TO SOMEONE WITH ASPERGER'S/HFA*

Ranking of issue by stress caused

Percent of respondents living with issue

#1 Anxiety 98%
#2 Self-esteem/self-identity 95%
#3 Aversion to change 87%
#4 Meltdowns 87%
#5 Depression 87%
#6 Sensory issues 86%
#7 Making and keeping friends 86%
#8 Personal management issues 85%
#9 Intimacy, dating, sex and marriage 85%
#10 Emotional availability 85%
#11 Faking it 84%
#12 Getting and keeping a job 83%
#13 Disclosing a diagnosis 79%
#14 Bullying 77%
#15 Choosing a career 76%
#16 Empathetic attunement 75%
#17 Being diagnosed 67%

Aversion to change 87%
Anxiety 86%
Meltdowns 83%
Sensory issues 83%
Making and keeping friends 82%
Self-esteem/self-identity 80%
Emotional availability 80%
Faking it 78%
Intimacy, dating, sex and marriage 77%
Depression 76%
Disclosing a diagnosis 73%
Personal management issues 72%
Bullying 72%
Getting and keeping a job 69%
Being diagnosed 61%
Choosing a career 58%
Empathetic attunement 58%

*Based on proprietary research conducted by Craig R. Evans in 2012–2013. See Appendix for more information.

Chapter One

Anxiety

Chapter One — Anxiety

> **"Why would a diagnosis be important for my twelve-year-old daughter?"**

CRAIG: "Dr. Tony, we have your book on anxiety and we feel strongly that such therapy is needed for our kids. However, we live in an isolated area, where there's limited access to professionals who are trained in cognitive behavioral therapy and children on the spectrum. Do you have any other ideas on how we can access this help? Have you ever heard of parents doing a group, using your anxiety resource or other resources to work on this as laypersons?"

DR. TONY: Brilliant! Do it! All I can say is when I wrote my anxiety book, *Exploring Feelings*, I didn't write it to be exclusively used by clinical psychologists. Interestingly, the university that did the orig-

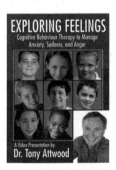

inal evaluation subsequently did a study of parents using the book without a psychologist, and it was just as good.

DR. TONY: I think parents know their kids. Parents aren't stupid, and they have a reasonably good idea of what to do. I don't think that as a parent, you're barred from using the programs; they're logical, they're common sense. It would be great if you had a clinical psychologist but if you don't, this is too important to abandon. As laypersons, you are not excluded from the ability to use programs, and if you haven't got other resources, do it.

"Coping with the death of a loved one."

CRAIG: "I am in therapy with a psychologist for anxiety disorders. Some weeks ago, my therapist told me that I may have some ASD traits, and I have questions. How do people with Asperger's react to and cope with life difficulties like chronic diseases, or events like the death of a significant person? Can these challenges, especially when they add up, increase social problems?"

DR. TONY: Well, the answer very quickly is, "Yes, they can." But I'm going to go through a number of things on that question. When we look at chronic diseases, one of the factors in ASD is going to be pain sensitivity, and often those with ASD may not report pain in the way that other people do. Whenever someone with an ASD said they've got pain, I take it very seriously. There's something probably going on there. Under stress, whether emotional stress or physical distress, the features of ASD usually increase: more social withdrawal, greater sensitivity to certain events, and more rigid thinking.

When the person is stressed, we get an increase in ASD characteristics and the person has difficulty reporting what's the matter. Often, a relative who knows that person may give the doctor a lot more information than the person with ASD can. It's not necessarily a linguistic problem, but a self-reflection problem.

Chapter One — Anxiety

The other topic was in relation to the death of a significant person, and here the reaction can be unconventional. That leads others to feel that the person doesn't care, but it's just a different way of coping. When death occurs, first, I must explain to the person with ASD that other people will become extremely emotional. They may burst into tears and look extremely distressed, and the person with ASD needs to know the answer to, "What do I do? Do I leave them alone? Do I make them a cup of tea?" To those who may be showing signs of despair in grieving, I say, "Please tell the person with ASD, 'I'm okay. What I'd like you to do is give me a hug, then I'll feel better.'" Their own way of grieving is going to be different and, again, can involve an increase in ASD features.

We would expect a greater withdraw, as the person is not good at disclosing their inner feelings and thoughts to other people. They're not going to use affection, disclosure, or conversation as their way of coping, which means the grieving process is going to take longer and the person is also going to have their times of distress. They may cope with it by solitude. Relatives and partners may say, "He's gone away for the weekend, no contact." The person is readjusting and recalibrating their life, but they're doing it by going offline, which could be very worrisome for other people.

There may not be the tears that you would expect, but there may be an increased amount of focus on a special interest as a thought blocker to stop those grieving thoughts from coming through. When you know ASD, it's very logical and appropriate, but others misinterpret what's happening.

Ask Dr. Tony

> **"My Asperger's boyfriend's mother died. Now he doesn't want to hear from me."**

CRAIG: The next question is, "My boyfriend of many years was recently diagnosed with Asperger's, and he just lost his mother. He broke up with me days after the funeral. He took off traveling and he doesn't want to hear from me. He's convinced he's acting on what he needs to do because he's learned now that life is short. Is there any way to help him realize that running away won't fix the hurt?"

DR. TONY: That tells me a lot about how you cope with grief: to share the feeling and use affection, support, and conversation as your way of cleansing the system and overcoming that sense of grief. It's an interpersonal way. That's the usual way for neurotypicals; we share and cry together. In Asperger's, alleviating distress, confusion, and change is done internally and in solitude. It's quite likely that he has left not necessarily as a rejection of Jane, but really to sort himself out on his own. Solitude is emotionally restorative, but the trouble is this can take a lot of time. By being alone, he's adjusting to the new situation and overcoming his sense of grief. Those with Asperger's tend to grieve in a very different way than neurotypicals, which leads to accusations like, "What are you doing? You don't care." I think he may be going beyond the usual circle of contacts to sort himself out.

CRAIG: He needs time alone.

Chapter One — Anxiety

"My thirty-one-year-old ASD son with learning disabilities is having trouble understanding the deaths of his grandparents."

CRAIG: The next question relates to understanding the death of a loved one: "I have a thirty-one-year-old son with autism, he also suffers from learning disabilities. His mental age is six to seven and he has epilepsy. Although his seizures are medicated, they remain uncontrolled. He has reacted very badly to the death of his maternal grandparents. He refuses to go outdoors and he worries when I or my wife leave the room. He's also losing any interest in life.

"We've tried *Social Stories*™ to explain their deaths but he doesn't understand what is being drawn or told. I feel that some of his seizures are anxiety-driven rather than epilepsy-driven. We still

believe he's in grief. All his sensory-sensitive areas seem to be much more heightened and they're getting worse. Is there anything you can suggest for us to try?"

DR. TONY: In autism and Asperger's, the grief reaction is going to be different and unconventional. Neurotypicals can work through their grief by sharing their feelings, crying together, and talking about their loved one. That group therapy of shared grief allows us to move through it much faster. For those with ASD, the grief leads to an increase in ASD features as their way of coping (greater social withdrawal, engagement in a special interest, etc.). It's going to take a long time to come to terms with that grief.

There's also that sense of loss which can lead to a reactive depression and fear of losing other people. If that loved one went to a hospital, for example, it is determined that hospitals are where people die, and they'll be scared about going to a hospital themselves or of other people going.

Jessica Kingsley Publishers have published two or three books on grief and autism, I would recommend looking into some literature. He's going through a recognition of his intense emotions and has difficulty in expressing those. It's going to take, I would estimate, two to three years at least to come through it.

"How do I help my fourteen-year-old, high-functioning ASD son deal with the loss of his dad?"

CRAIG: "I'm looking for some advice on how to help my fourteen-year-old, high-functioning ASD son deal with the loss of his dad, which happened two weeks ago. My other two kids will talk about their feelings, write, or create to get it out in a different way. My HFA son mostly just paces and asks rapid-fire questions, not about his dad's death or his dad—just about anything that will keep his mind busy. The pamphlets the funeral homes sent home with us on 'how to help your grieving child' just don't fit him. Do you have any concrete suggestions on how to help him?"

Chapter One — Anxiety

DR. TONY: The two other children have neurotypical ways of responding to grief. They share the emotion, express it with tears, and have the ability to alleviate their grief and thereby come to terms with it fairly quickly. Now for many with ASD, crying may be a rare event and it may not be their way of expressing despair. What will occur is an increase in autism spectrum behaviors.

When your son asks all those questions and paces, those are his ways of alleviating negative emotions. The pacing is a sort of ritualistic action to calm him down when he's distressed. He's using the rapid-fire questions as a sense of reassurance and, as you said, to keep his mind busy. In other words, they're a thought-blocker from those negative emotions. That means that your son is going to take a lot longer to come to terms with the grief and change.

When this occurs, you may need to explain to him through a Social Story™ why other people are so distressed and what he's expected to do in response. Otherwise, he's  not only lost his father, but people seem upset and they're giving off signals that he doesn't understand or know how to respond to. You can say, "When you see Mom or your siblings crying, please give them a hug. They would really appreciate it." Once he does, make sure to say, "Oh, thank you. That really made me feel much better." This way he has a sense of knowing how to respond to your grief.

Be prepared for him to take a lot longer to come to terms with his own emotions; others do it by talking, but that's not his way. Drawing is sometimes a possibility. You may find an increase in intensity of a special interest as a thought blocker. People need to be aware that his way of coping with the grief will be to internalize it rather than share it, and that he may display more ASD features. They are temporary, but may last months.

Ask Dr. Tony

CRAIG: "My twenty-four-year-old sister continues to suffer emotional flashbacks from several anxiety-producing doctor visits. During these visits, her anxiety went so high that it overwhelmed her ability to answer questions appropriately. Now, she deeply regrets these incidents and she's become self-deprecating over them. She calls herself an idiot or stupid for her unusual behavior, which was clearly brought on by the stress. This negative self-esteem issue is alarming. Is this post-traumatic stress disorder? She's on medication for anxiety but it doesn't appear to be helping. More importantly, what can we do to help her?"

Dr. Tony: This anxiety-driven selective mutism is a common characteristic, more so in women with Asperger's than the men. They get so anxious, they freeze and can't speak. In severe anxiety, the three responses are fight, flight, or freeze. She may have frozen and gotten tongue-tied, tripped over words, or couldn't speak; but that's due to anxiety, not stupidity.

The next thing she's done is blame herself. That comes from past experience of other people being critical of her, she's internalized the criticism of a peer group or teacher. Her reaction is to blame herself and she shouldn't do that.

This is a bit similar, but it's not a classic PTSD: it's more of an anxiety issue that's occurred here. What can be done to help? I think explaining why she couldn't speak, that it's not a sign of stupidity, and she shouldn't self-blame. Also, if she has to go to a doctor again, make sure she has an opportunity to relax and take her time to explain her difficulties. It's a learning experience. Next time she goes to a doctor, she should have someone with her that could keep her calm and speak for her if she feels tongue-tied.

Craig: Excellent.

Dr. Tony: Also, I would recommend what I do whenever I have a clinic appointment: I always record our conversation. The person with Asperger's goes away with a full record of everything we went through, so that they don't have to rely on verbal or auditory memory of what I say.

"Sometimes my eight-year-old daughter says things she knows aren't accurate. She wants me to correct her. Why?"

CRAIG: The next question is from an HFA mother. It says, "I'm a mother of an eight-year-old girl who is high-functioning. She is able to communicate, however, communication with her is limited. She's quite well adapted to school. There are two main problems with her. First, she is obsessed with schedules. Once a week, on Friday, I do shopping with her to teach her how. Every day I hear that she says she wants Friday now.

"The second thing is her compulsive behavior. She often says something to hear that she is wrong, such as, 'Mom, I really want to drive a car now.' At lunchtime she might say, 'I want chocolate now.' My question to Dr. Tony is about interpretation of such behavior and tips on how to cope with them."

DR. TONY: I'll be cautious of overanalyzing or interpreting that. In anxiety, there can be a desire for prediction. Some with classic autism will turn a light switch on and off, or ask what time it is. They know the time, however, what they want is reassurance of a predictable answer from the person. They just want you to confirm because they're needing a sense of reassurance and being right.

When your daughter does this, it can be a cue that she's feeling stressed about something but can't describe what it is. She has prompted communication in what I call a "foreign phrase dictionary."

When she asks those questions, which seem bizarre, it may be her way of saying, "I'm worried about something. Please help me." Don't over-focus on the question. Just say to your daughter, "That seems to tell me you're upset about something or stressed. Let's have some quality time together. Let's relax. Let's do something that makes you feel better." Rather than get entangled with answering the question, use them as a cue she's distressed.

"How do I help my stepson deal with his chronic pain?"

CRAIG: The next question has to do with living with pain. "My thirty-one-year-old stepson has been diagnosed with Asperger's in the last few years. He also suffers from chronic pain. My partner and I need some tools to help him cope, as he catastrophizes the pain and he suffers from anxiety and depression. He's unable to work or socialize and we want to try to help him understand what the doctors are telling him."

DR. TONY: The anxiety is probably amplifying the pain. The anticipation of pain will make him more anxious, and the more anxious he is the more pain he will perceive. He may need to learn to relax, and that could be done through yoga and meditation. There are a whole range of things that could help him feel calmer. When he's calmer and more relaxed, he may be more able to cope with the discomfort and pain. I have had some success (strangely enough) in referrals to hypnotherapists who specialized in pain management. If you have a hypnotherapist who seems to have an understanding of autism, they may be able help that person cope with pain through hypnosis.

Chapter One — Anxiety

> **"I have PSTD and ASD. I'm having trouble dealing with intrusive thoughts."**

CRAIG: The next question is, "How do I deal with disturbing intrusive thoughts? I have PTSD from finding my husband after he killed himself. I cannot get the intrusive pictures of what I saw out of my mind. It's getting worse and causing more and more disruption in my life. None of my usual coping skills are working. How can I help myself?"

DR. TONY: This is a new area for research: PTSD and ASD. Unfortunately, many people with ASD have suffered trauma in some way, either malicious trauma from others or they've witnessed something traumatic. There are people who specialize in PTSD, but they may or may not know about autism spectrum disorders. We're looking to try and develop professionals with expertise in both areas.

I met someone in Australia recently who is specializing in this area with some degree of success. I'm not an expert in PTSD, but I do know that whichever strategies are used need to be modified for the ASD mindset—difficulty converting thought and emotion into speech, intrusive images which can be incredibly upsetting, and a difficulty with closure after events, for example. These need to be gone through with someone who can provide you with help. I hope you can access someone with PTSD and ASD training.

Ask Dr. Tony

Dr. Tony on Dealing with Anxiety

Presented at the Flying High with Autism Conference – 2014

DR. TONY: One thing those with ASD are very good at is worrying. The survey that was done for the book *Been There. Done That. Try This!* suggests 86 percent of ASD adults have great concern with anxiety. As Richard McGuire said in his essay, "It might be a constant companion." When you've got intense chronic anxiety, you start to develop coping strategies. As Anita Lesko says, "There's a sixth sense of expectation of negativity." You're almost constantly hyper-vigilant waiting for the next negative experience, and that is exhausting. Note that exhaustion also contributes to being depressed.

When we look at strategies to manage anxiety, what I call the "distractive strategies," they are becoming either a control freak or avoidant: you want to control your experiences. That may include becoming quite dominant, or avoiding certain situations because you know that anxiety is going to be incredibly painful. Neurotypicals find it difficult to understand this because they don't have the same degree and depth of anxiety. Other destructive strategies are routines and rituals. They are soothing, comfortable, and predictable, and because they alleviate anxiety and stress, one of the problems is going to be enormous resistance to anything interfering with that. Basically, I say, "When the routines are taking over your life, you need help and treatment for anxiety." Another strategy is an emotional explosion, it sort of "cleanses" the system. I call it "rebooting the emotion computer."

There is another destructive strategy, and that is alcohol and/or drugs. What alcohol and drugs have done is create a safe bubble of indifference. It's a level of relaxation they've likely never experienced before, and it is incredibly dangerous. I do not recommend self-medication by those strategies.

Chapter One — Anxiety

There must be some constructive strategies, so what can we do? Two things, in particular, amaze me; one is physical activity. Often those with Asperger's main interests are sedentary, looking at a screen. That lethargy, unfortunately, is not a good idea. One of the best ways to manage anxiety is physical activity. As one person said, "Running keeps anxiety away." Please get a personal trainer or find someone who can help you with your personality and body type so that you can develop regular physical activity. It's one of the best treatments—better than medication and better than psychotherapy. The importance of diet amazed me, too. There were consistent responses that a diet free of junk food and full of nutrition seem to improve mood to no end. Whether this is linked to the toxic effects of junk food or something to do with Asperger's metabolism, I don't know.

I would also recommend relaxation and meditation. Psychologists are becoming more aware of mindfulness yoga. There are books on this that are written by people with Asperger's syndrome who said, "This has significantly improved my quality of life and reduced my anxiety." I do recommend you seriously have a look at meditation.

This next strategy works, but just be cautious about it: the use of a special interest as a thought blocker. When you're anxious, you get intrusive thoughts and worries, and one way of keeping those at bay

is to become engrossed in a special interest so you can't feel anxious. The interest is an energizer and it's also a source of pleasure. It works, but as with many things that work, use it in moderation and not as your primary way of alleviating anxiety.

Another tactic is being around animals, a safe person, or especially in nature (that may be a beach, a woodland, or a park in the city). There is something soothing and relaxing about being in nature, and those with Asperger's seem to be very in tune with that. Older, more mature people with Asperger's have said they tolerate and accept anxiety, but don't let it control their lives. Maturity may mean there is less of an emotional reaction.

Chapter Two

Self-Esteem/Self-Identity

Chapter Two — Self-Esteem/Self-Identity

"Home schooling or public education? Which is best?"

CRAIG: The next question is by a member of Autism Hangout and she has an eleven-year-old son with ASD. Like most kids who are trying to be mainstreamed, this woman is lamenting the fact that her son happens to be in a class with twenty other students and there's still only two aides in the class. She fears her son is falling through the cracks, as many parents do, and so she's asking, "Should I remove him from school and home school him, thereby cutting him off from any social contact with other school children, or should I possibly keep him in class and keep hoping for a change in the classroom situation?" Dr. Tony, what's your opinion?

DR. TONY: I'd like to spend an hour about this topic. Whatever decisions you make, I do strongly recommend that the child himself is involved in the actual decision making. I would normally have a sheet of paper with "public schooling" on one section and "stepping back for a year" on the other, listing positives and negatives of each. Then go through it with the child, and list what he and the family (and perhaps educators) think are the advantages and disadvantages of each option. He needs to be part of the decision making for his own integrity and in support of the final decision.

I know several children who have been home schooled, many of whom have had very beneficial results. It is important that the

person does socialize; it doesn't have to be with someone born six months either side of their birthday, as long as they've been home schooling and have had the opportunity to be with and relate to people. The main thing is that if they sometimes relate to people, it's a positive experience. On the other hand, keeping your son back a year might make him feel that it was due to intelligence or that he wasn't smart enough. We don't like that idea.

At this stage, he's stuck between the devil and the deep blue sea, it's hard to know which option would be best. Discussing each of those with the child is a good start.

> **"I'd rather have our son chunky and happy than starving himself to death."**

CRAIG: This question is about getting other family members to accept ASD behaviors. "My seventeen-year-old son was diagnosed with autism. Recently, my husband pointed out to me that he is gaining weight and he put the blame on me for buying too much food, setting out too much food, and then letting my son serve himself at meals. I told my husband that we must approach this matter delicately because of my son's tendency to become obsessed with things. I know there's a real danger of him developing an eating disorder because something similar happened about two years ago. Thankfully, it resolved itself without any intervention. I told my husband that I'd rather have our son chunky and happy than starving himself to death. Am I wrong in this thinking?"

DR. TONY: I think in that description there's a keyword: happy. It may well be that this person, at seventeen, has few pleasures in life. One of those pleasures is enjoyment of food. The trouble is, of course, if he is eating too much and increasing in weight, it has all sorts of medical and psychological issues. I would focus very much on broadening his pleasure experiences away from food (and possibly Internet games) into other areas of pleasure and happiness.

Also, he needs to work on the concept of self: the question, "Who am I?" This can help to make him aware of his physique as a way of portraying who he is to other people and to give him a degree of self-confidence and resilience, rather than to have comfort in food due to low self-esteem. If you're going to work on this problem there needs to logic coming from someone with expertise and credibility. Someone like a physician needs to talk to him about the long-term consequences—at seventeen, he probably thinks he's immortal. Excessive weight is going to affect his thinking abilities, his ability to move, and even to enjoy aspects of life. The key is happiness. He needs other sources of happiness.

"I'm an Aspie and proud of it. I would like to be a mentor. How would I go about starting a group?"

CRAIG: "Hi, Dr. Tony. I have a six-year-old son diagnosed with AS, and recently I have confirmed that I also have AS. I have been looking for a mentor program here in Darwin, with the hope that I might find someone who my son can relate to. However, there's nothing available here. Now that I know that I'm an Aspie (and I'm proud of it!), I would like to become involved in getting a mentor program started.

"I have researched. However, there are so many types of mentor programs that have been useful. I'm unsure as to how this program should look, how I should go about getting involved, or getting one of these things started. Can you help with suggestions?"

DR. TONY: Good question. I think we need to find out what your skills and qualities are and what you'd like to do to help someone. Then you contact a local newspaper or local radio, ask to be interviewed, and describe what you are going to do. Then people will have a way to contact you if they think that you could help them.

CRAIG: Very good.

DR. TONY: Include a newspaper article, a nice picture, a description of Asperger's, how it affects you and your son, the sorts of things that you can help with, and just say, "I'd like to help from my experience. We can work together on this. Please contact me." Include your email address and go through the media.

"Suicide is not an option."

CRAIG: "People with Asperger's syndrome, especially younger people, don't have the wisdom of somebody that has lived a life on a spectrum and seen that it does actually get better. How do you tell

Chapter Two — Self-Esteem/Self-Identity

people on the spectrum to deal with the depression that can lead to suicide? How do you tell them suicide is really a non-option?"

DR. TONY: "What a waste of talent. If you went, we'd all miss your abilities. Asperger's gives you a talent, and it's God's waste if you've been granted that and you throw it away because it's a different way of thinking. You've got talents! You may not have realized them yet, but they're there, we'll find them and develop them, which will give you a sense of self-worth. Because if you feel you don't have any self-worth, you have no self-respect. And there's no sense of value.

"These are painful aspects of life, the way people approach you, the way you think you're not going to be successful in your ambitions. That leads you to depression. In other words, your depression is a sensible reaction to your predicament. Anybody in their right mind would also feel depressed in that situation. You've got to change the way you look at this problem; it's the way you perceive it. There are particular qualities that you've got. Go through how they could be used to achieve success."

One of the major problems is that the person has absorbed criticism through childhood from peers and teachers and believed it. You have to say, "Change the logic. Why would they say that? Because they don't understand you, they enjoyed hurting you, but you've absorbed it. You didn't react, but that was a poison that stayed within you. We've got to get rid of that poison. We've got to explain why you were targeted using logic. It's because they wanted to show off to other kids—it wasn't anything to do with you. You've internalized it and blamed yourself. They didn't care who you were, they just found you an easy target."

It's nothing that can be cured within a couple of sessions. It takes a major paradigm shift of looking at the person more positively. That's why it's crucial, because otherwise we'll lose someone.

What I have found helpful when dealing with teenagers going through this is the support from other teenagers with Asperger's.

They give them advice and say, "Yeah, I know, that's how you feel now. I felt that way. It's intense but it will go away, there will be changes." It's a combined effort by psychologist, psychiatrist, and peers with Asperger's.

What I eventually want to develop is a psychotherapy for Aspies, by Aspies. I'm delighted that some Aspies now are going into psychology and psychotherapy. All the psychotherapy models are based for neurotypicals. I'm now finding I have colleagues with Asperger's syndrome and I'm very confident to pass on my clients to that person because I know they have credibility. They, too, have been through it. And Aspies know a fake, they know somebody who's just trying to cheer them up. They'd prefer someone who has been through a similar experience. That's convincing.

> **"Can too much parental protection be detrimental to our son's development?"**

CRAIG: Next question, "My husband and I have always arranged to be with our nine-year-old Aspie son anywhere he goes, school being an exception. I have seen our role (besides protector) as a type of facilitator. My friends think this isn't good, but our son is not successful in social situations on his own. Our son is very comfortable with one of us being there, is this detrimental to his development in a way that we're not seeing? Please advise, and thank you for all you do for our wonderful Aspies."

DR. TONY: Keep doing it! I think what you should do is ask your son to decide. Ask him if he'd like you to be there, and if he says he would, then you go. Over time, you can gradually pull back and simply be present: sometimes you're just reading a magazine or chatting to other people. I think you're a security blanket to reduce his anxiety. If he is tense and insecure, he won't be able to focus on the social element of what he's doing. You are a life raft and you are support, if he wants you there you should be there.

Chapter Three

Aversion to Change

Chapter Three — Aversion to Change

Creating a "foreign phrase dictionary."

CRAIG: Our next question says, "I'm an adult with a diagnosis of Asperger's syndrome and ADHD tendencies. Due to reasons beyond my control, my support providers have changed at the beginning of February. The thought of a major disruption in the structure of daily life stresses me out. For those who are going through similar situations of stress, what would you advise?"

DR. TONY: One of the major causes of distress for those with ASD is change, but especially change in people. Neurotypicals have an understanding of different types of people and can read their body language and gestures fairly easily. For a person with Asperger's, each new person is like a new species: they have their own facial expressions, style, and mannerisms.

This means that when an Aspie meets new people, they've got a whole new personality, a whole new structure, and a whole new atmosphere to adjust to. It is so stressful for them that we try and minimize as much change as possible. It's also important that when the new people come into the picture, they are good at understanding the person with ASD. Not everyone can do that—it's a two-way process and the person with Asperger's or autism has their own mannerisms. Those who know them well can read their body language, their subtle movements, and know what mood they are in. There's going to be a breakdown in communication right from the beginning. No wonder it's incredibly stressful for this person.

What we can do here is recognize what's involved. I sometimes ask those with Asperger's to create a "foreign phrase dictionary." In other words, "When I display a certain mannerism, this is what I'm thinking and feeling." Sometimes working with the parent or the last care workers can be beneficial. Ask them to write down how they "read" the individual, how to recognize their moods, how to determine what they're thinking and feeling. That way, it can be passed on to the new person in a document that allows them to translate: "Ah, when you start talking about this topic, it really means that you're worried about something else. When you look at me with that slightly changed facial expression, I read that as sadness, but in fact, you're just okay." That information needs to be passed on.

"How can I motivate my AS son? Can I improve his focus?"

CRAIG: "Dear Dr. Tony, I am the mother of a seven-year-old son with AS. He is academically very bright but clearly lacks social skills. I have two questions about him. The first is, how do I motivate him to complete his work? Even though I know he is capable, he keeps putting off his schoolwork. The second question is, is there a way I can improve his focus? He can focus on topics in his interest over long periods, but not on things that he's not interested in."

Chapter Three — Aversion to Change

DR. TONY: This is a common one. He's very bright but very dedicated to what he's particularly interested in, and he'll probably describe the other activities at school as boring. People with Asperger's are very black and white, they either like something or they don't. Typical kids know things like, "The passing grade is 40 percent. I'll just get 41 percent and I'm there." But those with Asperger's say, "I don't like it. I don't want to do it. What's the use of it? I'm not going to waste my time on it, because I've got far more interesting things to do." It's a tricky situation, he's only seven years old.

If you can, get the teacher to weave aspects of his special interest into the task. If the kid doesn't like the social side, for example, and the teacher presents in a group in the classroom, maybe the child can learn by reading in a textbook or on a computer. If you can take away the classroom environment and have him sit in a corner or in the library to read, then present to the class as an expert, he becomes a teacher.

Now, how can one improve his focus? You've got to remember that he needs short breaks. Recognize that every so often, he's going to drift off into his imagination or a distraction. Then you clear the decks and make sure that he's really going to focus on what's at hand. There may be kids nearby who can prompt him to get back to work.

"How do we tell our eighteen-year-old son that it's time to move on?"

CRAIG: "Our son is now eighteen, and we're having a very hard time convincing him that it's time to move to the next level. He spends most of his time online gaming and chatting with friends all over the country. He works two evenings a week, he sleeps during the day, and he hardly eats. How can we help him move forward?"

DR. TONY: If it's the closure of school and there's a whole new adult life ahead of him, he doesn't have the clear structure or purpose that he had at school. On one hand, he's wanting to be independent. On the other, he's finding pleasure in spending time with things that he enjoys in the freedom of not going to school. Getting on to the next level—employment—is so important for those with Asperger's syndrome. It supplies structure in their day, a sense of self-worth, income, and so on.

He works two evenings a week (which is good, but that's not enough), he sleeps during the day, and hardly eats. In adolescence, one thing that can happen with Asperger's is a switching of the day and night cycle. These are part of his sleep issues. He's a night owl and that may be the time when his body says, "You are at your most able to learn and concentrate," even though it's at the opposite of what one is expected to do. He may need to go to a sleep clinic to see if they can recalibrate the sleep system.

Help him move forward through his interests and his peers; he's got to feel successful. I do feel for the family in that sense. The way out may not be through them, but through his interests. He should get out and find a job involved in his interests.

"How can one best motivate an Aspie?"

CRAIG: The next questions are from people who love people on the spectrum. "How can one motivate an Aspie to complete work and improve focus on things that don't interest them?"

DR. TONY: One thing that motivates those with Asperger's is success! There's a pathological fear of making a mistake but also an

Chapter Three — Aversion to Change

enormous delight in getting it right. They may need more positive feedback of how well they've done. One of the other issues is that they find it very difficult to switch from one activity to another if the first activity isn't completed. They have a compulsion for completion.

Also, they may look at the outcome from their personal perspective rather than the priority of other people. There are many components here. When it comes to motivation, identify when you could suggest they start something. It has to be the natural close of a particular activity. Give them positive feedback of what they have done correctly but also say, "Okay, from your perspective you want to finish on the computer and to get to level three. From my perspective, we need to go get the groceries from the supermarket, drop our daughter off at the daycare, and go and get some money from the cash dispenser. You're good at math, which takes more time? That's why we have to go."

It requires a partner to explain and accept the priorities and expectations of the partner with Asperger's, but to then say, "We need to do this, this, and this. This outweighs your priorities, that's why I'm asking you to do it." Another thing that motivates people with Asperger's syndrome, of all ages, is that they have no room for errors. I mentioned the need for more reassurance, but there's also the intrinsic enjoyment of doing something well. Other kids will ask themselves what their reward is for doing something. Those with Asperger's seem to think, "I've made no mistakes." It's the intrinsic reward of success, rather than the delight of other people.

Chapter Four

Meltdowns

Chapter Four — Meltdowns

"Our five-year-old, non-verbal child gets aggressive and hurts her sister. What can we do?"

CRAIG: "Hello Dr. Attwood, do you have any suggestions on how to handle my five-year-old? She is very large for her age, and very strong. She is non-verbal. She has periods of very severe aggression during which she pinches, scratches, hits, kicks, and pulls out clumps of her sister's hair (I think you get the picture). We started her on medication, hoping to curb some of her obsessive tendencies and perhaps even calm her down. She has been calmer overall, but she's still obsessive and she's also quite destructive to her home. There seems to be no change in the aggression, either. We can never quite read her. During aggressive periods, I do try to give her acetaminophen presuming that she is in pain. We just started a home therapy program but I'm sad to say that we don't even like this kid anymore. What else can we do?" First off, don't feel bad about being stressed out. Dr. Attwood?

DR. TONY: That's a very important question, one that I have in my clinical experience almost every week. One of the interesting things is that kids with autism do tend to be larger. She is a five-year-old, non-verbal. You use the term aggression. I'm a bit cautious of using that term. I strongly suspect that the root cause is actually anxiety and panic.

There may be a feeling of anger or frustration because a compulsion or something that she anticipates is not occurring. In a way, she might be having panic attacks rather than being aggressive. She is trying to survive and cope in her world. This is her way of getting her message across and saying, "The anxiety is so intense, I must end it!" The only way she knows how to stop that person or make them do something is to attack.

We need to observe her and help build her communication system. We need to find out the things she wants to communicate and make them happen in her life by choices. We need a system in pictures that she can use to understand what is going to happen, when, with whom, and for how long. Once she understands the sequence, she then knows what is going to happen rather than impose what she wants to occur. If it doesn't happen, she uses control or manipulation as a survival mechanism.

We also need a program to help her release her energy and agitation in a more constructive way. As she is five, I would strongly recommend programs to encourage her to learn how to relax; I would see this as speech pathology in communication. She needs a way of alleviating what I think is confusion in a changing world. She needs to understand the pattern of life and an effective communication system to prevent these meltdowns.

CRAIG: It's clear you have many, many years of experience in this field.

DR. TONY: Thirty-five years! [laughs]

> **"Sometimes I lose my ability to talk and I hit myself. What can I do?"**

CRAIG: "My ability to talk can go down at any time of the day and I'm left figuring out how I'm going to communicate my needs. My frustration comes out as hitting myself. I hit my head and my arms. I want to stop doing these things. How can I better my communication skills? What can I do or use to help me?"

DR. TONY: First of all, stop hitting yourself, that's going to do no good at all. It may be that your brain goes into a state of overload, which means that you just can't do anything. When that occurs, you've just got to go with it. Hurting yourself in frustration is not going to improve the situation and it's going to make recovery more elusive.

What you need to do is check if there are any signals that one of these meltdowns is on the way. When it is, you need to say to people, "Excuse me, but I'm heading into overload. I need to take a deep breath." Go to the restroom, close cubicle door, close your eyes, and just relax, because getting frustrated is no good for anyone.

"My rage attacks on myself are getting worse."

CRAIG: The next question is also from the same woman. She writes, "I get quite a lot of rage attacks. Rage attacks for me consist of getting angry at myself and very irritable, where I smash my room up and I hit my head and I punch my arms and I say I want to kill myself. The rage attacks are getting worse, I have seven incidences

of self-harming by cutting my arms. Sometimes I do it to ease my emotional pain and sometimes I do it just to feel alive. I am scared that one day I'm going to do something stupid." What would you say to her?

DR. TONY: You could have an accident and you could cut something serious. When you get these rage attacks, please tell someone. They may not be able to help you, but they can be with you. I wouldn't ask them to talk to you or do anything but just be there. That would be supportive emotionally but not intrusive, and if an accident occurs then they can quickly get medical help to deal with the injury.

The question regarding the rage attacks is, "Why?" Again, they're quite common and the intensity is unbearable. The self-injury could be for a variety of reasons and you explain this perfectly with, "Sometimes I do it to feel alive." It serves to actually get some recognition of yourself, or to ease the emotional pain by something else that's more painful and blocks the other emotional pain in your life.

It's become a coping mechanism for emotional experiences. You really need to talk to somebody who understands the issue of depression and self-esteem about this, so that you can identify the triggers that provoke a rage attack. Recognize when they're on their way and have an emergency procedure to live through it and recover afterwards. It's very important to talk to someone about these rage attacks and what's going through your mind at the time.

The rage can be misinterpreted as anger when, in fact, it's a depression attack. People need to understand that the person isn't necessarily aggressive, it's basically an intense emotion coming out. I don't know of a medication that will quickly resolve this, because the attacks come quickly and are very intense—sometimes too quick for any medication to work. It's best to have a plan for when one's on its way, an "emergency response."

Chapter Four — Meltdowns

It's like telling somebody, "I'm going to have a seizure. Watch out." Somebody's with you to check that you're okay when you come out of the seizure, and you need that for these attacks.

"Is there's a correlation between sensory-seeking behavior and self-harm?"

CRAIG: "I'm wondering if this is premeditated. Here's what happens to me, I feel like I get a sort of pressure building up inside of me that leads me to be a quite sensory-seeking. I may listen to painfully loud music, despite being quite sensitive to sounds normally. The pressure build-up can also lead me to bite or squeeze myself, or feel hunger in a painful sort of way. Ultimately, the pressure feelings culminate in self-harm with sharp objects. Is self-harm related to autism and sensory issues, and is there a solution?"

Explosion is OK but

Don't Damage! Find Diversion!

Meltdowns
Is Sensory Seeking Behavior and Self Harm Related?

Ask Dr. Tony

DR. TONY: Self-harm in ASD is caused for several reasons. One has just been described: the buildup of tension over time culminating in a meltdown. It seems that you can only have closure when you've done something quite dramatic. The self-harm releases that pressure and you get it over and done with. The problem is in psychological terms, it's self-reinforcing. It's what we call negative reinforcement. It ends an unpleasant feeling, like medicine with a headache.

You have the buildup of tension, you have the explosion, and then you're okay. You're more likely to use that strategy again because it gives you the "feel-good" factor. There's a buildup of pressure. You need to make it a controlled explosion, where you can find some diversionary activities or substitute physical activities that won't cut or bruise you. It may be jumping up and down. It could be all sorts of things. Talk with someone about what you can do to get it out of your system, but in a way that's not going to cause damage.

Now, there are three factors in self-harm. One is that self-harm is calming. When I ask someone with Asperger's what the feeling was like when they cut themselves they may say, "It's not pain, it actually helps me relax. It calms me down." That's concerning, because it then becomes a compulsion to reduce anxiety and stress.

The second reason is actually to create a physical pain as a means to block emotional pain. The third reason is self-hatred, or an expression of a depression attack. They may feel like they hate themselves, they can't control their mind, their body, their reactions, or their lives. Those are the three factors we explore when self-injury occurs in Asperger's.

> **"He gets violent during meltdowns. He can't express his feelings in words."**

CRAIG: "I have an eight-year-old son with Asperger's, dyslexia, and speech and language delays. I find it hardest when he goes into a meltdown and gets violent. He can't express his feelings in words yet and I can't get through to him at all. Tony, he is a unique, special boy and he means very much to me. Do you have any advice?"

DR. TONY: Yes. When he has the meltdown, don't ask him what's the matter because his eloquence will desert him. At that time of emotionality, he's not going to give you a coherent explanation or find the vocabulary. Here are some general hints for when he goes into meltdown; first of all, you must remain as calm as you can and say to him, "I'm not upset with you, angry with you, or disappointed, I'm just going to help you relax." Then, focus on verbiage such as, "Look, something's upsetting you, we don't know what it is. If you're calm, you're smart. Just calm down, take a deep breath." You may go through pleasant scenes, compliments of what he's done, or things that he's looking forward to but he's not missing out on because of his behavior.

Basically, you need to get that emotion back on an even keel. Then he'll be able to listen, explain, and can try suggestions of dealing

with it. The first thing you're going to do in those meltdowns is say, "Let's work together on calming you down." He needs to develop a vocabulary to describe his feelings; that's why we developed *The CAT-kit*— Cognitive Affective Training (available in the USA from Future Horizons)—which supplies a thermometer and toolbox to arrange strategies for those who lack eloquence in describing their feelings.

Afterwards, when he's had a meltdown, say, "We need to learn from this. On your thermometer, how strong was the feeling from zero to ten?" The kit contains a book that includes pictures or descriptions of all the things that agitate him, so you can go through the book and point to what was causing the problem. Then, go through another book of repair strategies to get him to feel better and deal with the situation.

"What type of discipline will an Asperger's child benefit from?"

CRAIG: "Our granddaughter has high-functioning autism or Asperger's. She will be nine years old very soon. We're having a hard time with discipline. What type of discipline will an Asperger's child benefit from?"

DR. TONY: The simple answer is, none. [laughs]

Chapter Four — Meltdowns

DR. TONY: When you make threats or attempt consequences in a meltdown, it's not going to work. At that stage, the person is in such an intense level of emotion that their frontal, logical-thinking mind has switched off. You can threaten them with chopping their fingers off. You can promise them one million dollars. It's going to make no effect; in a state of very intense emotion, consequences are not going to be cognitively processed. Now, this doesn't mean to say that there shouldn't be consequences ... but only when the meltdown is over and they can cope with them.

This is a very important question, because meltdowns can occur very early in a person's life and they continue if you're not careful. What I'm going to do is explain the nature of the meltdown and some strategies of what to do during them. Now, a meltdown is usually a sensory, social, or cognitive overload. Sensory would be too many bright lights, too much noise. Social is too many people. Cognitive is in terms of too much information. In these situations, the fuse blows and the person is completely lost in that intense experience.

Now, a strategy: most of the people reading this will have a GPS in their car or know what it is. I want you to imagine you're going to a destination, sitting next to your partner. You type in where your destination is and you follow the directions. It says, "At the next junction, turn left," but you're distracted and you go straight over the junction. Your partner shouts, "What do you think you're doing? We're going to be late. I should be driving. You don't know how to drive!" and has a meltdown.

Now, the GPS does not say, "What the devil do you think you're doing? I just told you to turn there. You don't know your left from your right. How many times have I got to tell you how to drive?" It doesn't focus on what you did wrong, it focuses on what to do right in a voice that's calming and reassuring. In the meltdown, it is very important not to focus on the damage or your feelings in that situation. Calmly, using your best GPS voice, repair the situation. That's my advice for a meltdown. Obviously, afterwards you may say, "Okay, we need to learn from this," and start off with the child's perspective. "From your perspective, *this* is the situation, right? Okay. Now, from my perspective, this is the situation. If you feel like you're about to lose it, I need to know because I can help you."

The answer is to help, not discipline. Once you reach a certain point, consequences and punishment aren't going to work. What works with ASD is logic. Also, prevention is better than a cure. You need to say, "Okay, I need to remember that when there are too many bright lights or too many people, you're sensitive and you could have a meltdown. I need to watch the situation. If you feel a sense of overload, please tell me a secret word or phrase like 'I can't cope.' Then we will go to a separate room, I'll ask you to close your eyes, and we will take a break from what's going on." That's my recommendation for meltdowns.

> *"I've been under a lot of stress at work and my urge to, for lack of a better term, 'throw a tantrum' is ever increasing."*

CRAIG: Next question: "I'm an adult who was recently diagnosed with AS and I'm having difficulty identifying and expressing my emotions. When I was a child, I reacted to negative emotions by screaming, kicking, and throwing things, and I usually felt much better shortly afterward. As an adult, I know that kind of behavior is inappropriate. The trouble is, I haven't learned another effective way to express emotions, instead, they build up and cause a lot of stress and anxiety. Recently, I've been under a lot of stress at work and my urge to, for lack of a better term, 'throw a tantrum' is ever increasing. I'm even having dreams at night in which I try to scream but I have no voice. Can you suggest any strategies for dealing with and expressing such complex negative emotions that work well for people with Asperger's?"

DR. TONY: First of all, don't inhibit it, go with it. Just make sure it's not in public or within the family. It's what I call "cleansing the system," or "rebooting the emotion computer." It's a quick fix that gets it out of your system and it's very healthy. The problem is, other people could be confused or scared by it. It needs to be done in private. You could also do a little bit of what we call "creative destruction," where you have a box of things that you can smash and crush for recycling. Once you've crushed those cans and that packaging and really get it out of your system, it's better than medication and it's quick. In other words, don't get upset by it or embarrassed. Throw a tantrum in private because it will work wonders, just make sure that other people know what you're doing so if they hear you screaming, shouting, and crushing things, they know that it's okay. The difficulty is, you can't really do that at work unless you go to the toilet, close the cubicle door, and then silently go through your rage with gestures and thoughts to get it out of your system. Then, open the cubicle door with a smile on your face and just flush the toilet.

CRAIG: [laughs]

DR. TONY: What you're doing is flushing all the anguish down the toilet.

CRAIG: Yes, excellent.

> **"I go into sensory overload ... I can't speak, feel dizzy and sick, and lose orientation."**

CRAIG: "I have a question regarding meltdowns. Sometimes when I suffer from sensory overload, I go into a kind of a trance similar to a computer freezing because too many windows are open. I lose my ability to speak, I have severe difficulties understanding speech, my vision is fuzzy, I feel dizzy, and sometimes sick. I also lose orientation, I can't take anything in and I'm lost in my own world where noise and light is even more unbearable than before. Is this a meltdown caused by sensory overload, or is it something else?"

DR. TONY: Yes, it sounds like it's an overload from sensory experience and basically your brain has blown a fuse. The thing is, you've got to get out of those situations as fast as you can, and often by reducing sensory experience and solitude you can slowly recover. There's an excellent book called *From Anxiety to Meltdown* by Deborah Lipsky where she describes what happens during a meltdown due to huge sensory overload.

You try to identify the situations where you're likely to experience overload, and make yourself aware when your sensory system is becoming overwhelmed. You can then either avoid the situation or try and take your mind off it through distraction. Some will use a computer game, but I also strongly recommend that you explain to people that you are overwhelmed by the sensory experience. Then, for a moment, take a deep breath and try and reduce the sensory experience.

Chapter Five

Depression

Chapter Five — Depression

"My negative moods are mostly triggered by his behavior."

CRAIG: The next question comes from an Autism Hangout member. She says, "Dear Dr. Tony, I am a woman diagnosed with clinical depression and I am married. Our marriage counselor believes that my husband has Asperger's syndrome. Everything I read about AS seems to fit him, although he refuses to acknowledge it. In addition, my individual therapist and I both believe that my negative moods are mostly triggered by his behavior. Typical of many wives of Aspie men, I suffer from feelings of isolation and lack of support from friends and family." Dr. Tony, she goes on to write that she's looking for ways that she will be able to express what she's dealing with to other loved ones, family members, and friends a bit more. Perhaps they can be a bit more empathetic to her situation. Are there any tools that you could suggest for her?

DR. TONY: Her husband may have what I call the Asperger's personality type, not the syndrome. It's a subclinical level that may only be apparent in the home environment. When that person is at work or at a social function of short duration, they may have a social rapport that is not suggestive of Asperger's syndrome.

However, those who know that person intimately and over time may realize that this is actually an exhausting process and many of

the other features of Asperger's syndrome are there. We have what we call the "Cassandra phenomenon." In Greek mythology, Cassandra has a gift of prophecy but the curse that no one will believe her. What can happen is you see those components at home, but other people will think you're crazy.

What you tend to get is a sense of loneliness. Often, ironically, the partner is an extreme socialite chosen by the person with Asperger's as social guidance: a maternal, caring, compassionate person who is very good at understanding his point of view, though he may not be good at understanding yours. The issue is going to be loneliness, affection deprivation.

When the person with Asperger's is upset with themselves or concerned about something, they tend to go inward, not sharing their concerns or emotions. They may get by with the capacity of affection that I call a cup, not a bucket. This particular woman may have the capacity of a bucket, and when she gets only a cup she feels depressed. This is very common for those with a partner with Asperger's syndrome. Now, there are a number of good books in this area published by Jessica Kingsley Publishers, and a new workbook for couples by Maxine Aston.

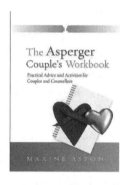

One of my concerns here is that other people may not believe her. What she needs to do is reach out to family members and friends who may understand and appreciate what she's going through.

For all Aspie partners: you do need support. You need a social life and to not feel guilty if your partner is not with you. You are enthralled and energized by socializing, but your partner is exhausted and worried by it. What happens is, you take on an Aspie lifestyle, and you may not like the sort of person you become. It's suitable for them to survive, but there's some essential component that's missing for you.

Chapter Five — Depression

He may not want a diagnostic assessment and he may not get one, because the severity of expression is not sufficient for psychological and psychiatric help. The diagnostic criteria, I'm afraid, are based on money—is it strong enough to warrant insurance funding for the psychologist and psychiatrist treatment? What this person does need is relationship counseling.

Asperger's and depression. "What can family do to help?"

CRAIG: "It seems that there's very little research dealing with depression in Aspies. Most of the techniques used to help are based on neurotypical chemistry. I've often wondered if this makes a difference, since a lot of these techniques are ineffective in Aspies. In my experience, external factors act as a trigger, but internal factors amplify and worsen the condition. Things like anxiety and overthinking also seem to make things much worse. Do you have any suggestions on dealing with depression and Aspies? Is there anything family or friends can do to help?"

DR. TONY: Very poignant and a very important at the moment. I've been designing a CBT program to treat depression in teenagers with Asperger's syndrome with my colleague and friend Michelle Garnett. We found it highly successful. The University of Queensland is now doing a randomized control trial with teenagers to see if it works. Next year, Michelle and I will be working on a program for adults with Asperger's and depression.

Now, the question relates to brain chemistry. I don't think it's necessarily brain chemistry that is different, but experiences ... and recognizing that the person with Asperger's has had much more bullying and teasing in their lifetime. One of the tragedies is that they have internalized the derogatory comments of their peers ("I am stupid, I am a loser,"). Whenever that person makes a mistake, they feel it just proves they're stupid; their thinking is very negative, which is often caused by their peer group. When you ask a person with Asperger's what they're feeling, they'll often reply, "I don't know." That's a short form for, "I don't know what thoughts are going through my mind. I can't grasp them and conceptualize them, but they're negative. I can't find the words."

That's such a complex sentence. They say, "I don't know." In other words, trying to grasp and describe internal feelings is very difficult, which means often the person tries to solve life's negative events themselves without sharing it or using affection or compassion as a way of alleviating feeling sad. There's also the issue of anxiety, they're worried about what might happen. Depression is thinking that whatever is going to happen, it's going to be bad. The two will produce over and over. It just goes on and on. When we look at this, there are major problems regarding depression and cognitive behavior therapy.

Chapter Six

Sensory Issues

Chapter Six — Sensory Issues

"High-pitched sounds hurt."

CRAIG: "I hate high-pitched sounds and when comes to high-pitched laughter, among other noises, I cringe like a scared child. It's been bothering me most likely since birth. Have you, Dr. Tony, looked into laughter as a sensory issue for those with Asperger's? Do you have any ideas as to how I could desensitize a sensory problem?"

DR. TONY: Oh, there's a lot in that question. First of all, it can be an issue of either a particular person's laughter or the pitch that is the sensory sensitivity. There can also be a psychological sensitivity in terms of a history of being laughed at. I have to explain to people with Asperger's (using *Social Stories*™) that there are many different types of laughter. They can be laughing with you or at the situation, but it's not necessarily ridicule. There's often a psychological element.

A suggestion could be to desensitize: use gradual exposure to the laughter and you eventually have the ability to tolerate it. In general, this tends not to work in Asperger's because the person doesn't habituate. They continually have a startled reaction to what's going on. Sometimes, the best way to handle this is to use a barrier; when

people laugh, cover your ears the best way you can. People have asked if hypnosis could work. It's a possibility!

Oh dear, I really feel for this person. I can't give a simple answer other than to create a barrier or use earplugs in this sort of situation. Then explain to them that you have a special hearing quality that makes some sounds a little bit like fingernails on a blackboard, and use that analogy. That says, "It's a sound that is absolutely excruciating for me."

"Why would someone be afraid to eat a salad?"

CRAIG: Here's another sensory question. "What is the deal with some Aspergians and salads? My grandson is afraid of salads and will not sit next to somebody who is eating one. Eggs seem to have the same effect. Is this normal for them? He won't touch fruits, salads, or vegetables."

DR. TONY: Welcome to autism and Asperger's! Your grandson is experiencing the sensory qualities. To you, what makes a good salad is the mixture of flavors and colors and textures. Those with ASD want either something fairly bland or consistent. A salad with so many ingredients is an explosion of taste, color, texture, etc. Neurotypicals find this absolutely delightful, but for those who have Asperger's it's far too much and overwhelming.

The same can go for vegetables and other foods. It can be some aspects of texture, taste, color, or many components that bother an ASD individual. You can encourage the child to be brave in trying various things, but I wouldn't force the child because it's a sensory issue that he's not going to be able to overcome by force. Sometimes you have to accept there are certain things they won't like. As time goes by, you may get them to add another little piece of lettuce (or other foods), but the important thing to remember is this is a painful experience, in a sensory sense. The person needs understanding and encouragement rather than a question of, "Well, why can't you eat it?"

"Are there four or five traits typical of people with Asperger's?"

CRAIG: This first question comes from someone who is fascinated by the whole spectrum of different personalities and characteristics of people with Asperger's. For instance, some can't stand heat. Some like cold, some can't stand cold. It goes the same way with volume and touch. His question is, "Are there four or five traits typical of people with Asperger's that run the gamut of the spectrum, one end to the other?"

TONY: A very good question. If we're looking at sensory sensitivities, for example, you get both hypersensitivity and hyposensitivity in the new diagnostic criteria (DSM-5). The hypersensitivity may be to certain sounds, but other sounds can hardly be heard. There may be a lack of sensation to touch but then on some occasions, there may be a light touch which is viewed as very painful.

CRAIG: This is all within the same person?

TONY: Yes. You can get that inconsistency across the sensory dimensions. It also occurs at the two extremes in other dimensions. When looking at social confusion, an individual can go down either of two paths; one is to become shy, introverted, or very cautious in social situations.

Others may do the opposite and become too intense and intrusive. The criticism may be either, "You need to come out of your shell more," or "You're too intense in what you do." You can get two extremes.

This inconsistency can also be seen in number skills. You can get some who are phenomenal with numbers, and others just have no clue.

There are some that are fascinated by reading or who are hyperlexic,

and yet there are others who are dyslexic. ASD is a condition that's very heterogeneous with many extremes. There's a lovely phrase, I didn't invent it: "When you've met a person with Asperger's, you've met one person with Asperger's." The heterogeneity, the variety of expression, I find fascinating.

CRAIG: The interesting thing is that so many people on the spectrum are now discovering that about themselves. In this diversity, there's just so much opportunity not only for hope, but for education for people at the same time.

TONY: Yes.

Chapter Six — Sensory Issues

CRAIG: I did read the other day that the occurrence of savant syndrome in people on the spectrum is one out of ten. Is that what you've read as well?

TONY: Yes. It's been known for some time. That means nine out of ten aren't, but it means that when you've got Asperger's syndrome, the savant characteristics, and high IQ, you've got genius. I'm trying to encourage people to use it if they've got it and to develop their skill, because we're all going to benefit. Whether it be art, music composition, science and information technology, designing new technological equipment … it's finding what that skill is and then developing it for a sense of self-identity and self-worth.

CRAIG: What you're saying is pursue your passion.

TONY: Absolutely. Spoken by somebody who's very passionate about Asperger's. [laughs]

"Pressure changes make me cringe."

CRAIG: The next question is about characteristics of sensory issues. This person is frightened by flashing lights and loud noises, but he's also discovered something else. This is his question. "I feel pressure changes very strongly (things like closing the last door in a car after entering it, closing the last window in a moving car, or being in a train if it's entering or exiting tunnels) and it's unpleasant to the point that it makes me cringe, even while everyone else doesn't seem to mind. Is this typical of somebody with Asperger's?

TONY: Yes, indeed it is, it's a sensitivity to air pressure. We tend to think of the auditory, the visual, and the smell sensitivity. It can be vestibular or proprioception—where your body is in space, and all those factors. All the sensory systems can be affected to various degrees. This person has a sensitivity to air pressure that may be common for other people, but is painful to him. People need to recognize that it's genuine. The person's not whining; it's a genuinely aversive experience.

"Dealing with noises and acting normal takes energy."

CRAIG: "Hello, doctor. I am an Aspie in my final year of medical school. Because I can sit in my room and read for hours without losing focus, I do well in exams. I'm now working in ward and I hear all these machines and people talking and breathing. I have to remind myself to act normal in conversations. This takes a lot of energy. Sometimes, I sleep for twelve hours just to be able to get out of it again. Do you have any advice?"

DR. TONY: I'm assuming this person is a medical student and has not broadcast that he has Asperger's ... but what he may do is say he has a condition called hyperacusis. That means extraordinarily sensitive hearing. People will ask, "Hyperacusis, what's that?" "That means I can literally hear a pin drop. When a noise is tolerable for you, it's excruciating for me because I have very sensitive hearing."

I think it's one of those situations where you can take a fragment of ASD and use a term for that, hyperacusis, and explain it as a medical professional. You could say, "In my daily life, I can't inhibit it. I have a startled reaction every time. This means that sometimes I am overwhelmed by too much noise and I need to take a silent break." That may be quite understandable for the ward staff, nurses, patients, etcetera.

Chapter Six — Sensory Issues

Living with Autism
Dealing with Noises, 'Acting Normal' and How Best to Recharge?

"Toe walking."

CRAIG: "I'd like to know more about toe walking and if my daughter could stop through therapy."

DR. TONY: I have never been asked this question, but it's a fascinating one. The toe walking is usually seen in younger children. Typical kids toe walk occasionally, and they like bouncing around a bit. With autism, it can become a regular form of movement. In autism there is a popularity of trampolines, swings, horse-riding, and music, and the key theme through all that is rhythm.

Toe walking is almost like having your own trampoline; if the person finds that sense of rhythm is needed in their life, that's what they will create. Now, there can be other issues. One is tactile—some of the kids really don't like the sensation of socks on their feet, grass, or sand, and will go on their tiptoes to avoid the pressure in that area.

If it becomes a prolonged characteristic, surgery may be considered to stop it. What we're looking for is a sensory assessment to see what's going on. Is that the person needing rhythm? If so, sometimes listening to music through headphones will provide them with the rhythm instead. The problem with the toe walking is often the kid doesn't really recognize they're doing it. You need a signal: something to remind to the child, not in a critical sense, that they need to walk flat.

I find most kids grow out of it eventually. If the parents can be patient and look at the sensory elements, especially rhythm and tactile, that may explain it.

"ASD and Munchausen syndrome."

CRAIG: "My sister was seen recently by an infectious disease specialist for an infection that she had acquired in the hospital. The doctor has been unable to explain why my sister is so prone to infections while in the hospital. He pulled me out of the room and stated that autism and Munchausen syndrome go hand in hand. He then went back in the room and confronted my sister with his theory. It was a terrible situation. Is there a link between ASD and Munchausen syndrome? Also, how can one defend themselves against an argument in a 'he said, she said' situation?"

DR. TONY: Munchausen syndrome is where the person pretends to be ill for a variety of reasons. Often the actual diagnosis may appear elusive in medical examinations and that can cause temptation to assume that it's fabricated, the person is making it up. But it's a terrible accusation to say that someone who is ill is faking it; I'm very concerned that this would occur. Now, there's

Chapter Six — Sensory Issues

no link between autism and Munchausen syndrome. Sometimes, I think when the person can't find a medical reason they look for a psychological reason. I think I've got to go through this in a bit more depth.

A person with Asperger's syndrome can have a different sensory system, which includes the reception of pain. Pain is a medical way of reporting where the problem is and the nature of it. The person may not be able to give pain information accurately. Secondly comes the ability to describe themselves and how they're feeling; often in Asperger's there's a mind-body division and the person is not in touch with their body. They're not very good at reporting the symptoms, which confuses medical professionals. We also know that those with Asperger's can be incredibly stressed, so you're going to get stress-related disorders, and Asperger's and autism are also associated with autoimmune disorders. Those need to be looked at, too.

I think there's an issue of jumping to conclusion that it must be pretend, when in fact I think it needs further investigation to find out what's going on. Many with Asperger's in general hospitals find communicating the nature of ASD very difficult to medical staff. They must explain that they have a different perception of pain and sometimes have difficulty describing the feelings in their body, but are under extreme stress and need to be assessed in a way that is working rather than being accusatory.

Chapter Seven

Making and Keeping Friends

Chapter Seven — Making and Keeping Friends

"Young neurotypical friends of young Aspies are gold!"

CRAIG: This woman has three children: a nine-year-old son with Asperger's syndrome, a seven-year-old son, and a three-year-old daughter. She writes about her nine-year-old Aspie son, who is a third grader. Apparently, he's very bright and he's very social with one neurotypical best friend. The two of them have developed this very tight bond. At school, the staff is seeing a dependency between the two children. She is wondering if this is something she should be concerned about, with the implications being that eventually her son will have to find a new friend. What are your thoughts on this?

DR. TONY: I'm very concerned that the school must not stop this friendship. This is gold! This is platinum! This is the best gift that any child with Asperger's could possibly want. Please do not let the school destroy that. If it is mutually supportive, it is beneficial for them. You see, he's nine years old—it is typical of nine-year-old kids to have close friendships, they're learning trust. Instead of being superficial, this is becoming a really trusting friendship. This is worth its weight in gold, do not allow the school to separate them.

CRAIG: [laughs] That's the most adamant I've seen you!

DR. TONY: If he's got a good friend and they're supportive of each other, it's strongly useful for his self-esteem, protects him from bullying and teasing, and he learns more about the depth of friendship. Any parent of a kid with Asperger's wants that. Don't let the school get in the way.

CRAIG: Yes, we should all be so fortunate that our Asperger's children have friendships such as that because they develop so many wonderful skills from it.

DR. TONY: Yes, absolutely. I would recommend for this mom to talk to her son's friend and make good friends with him, too. Make her son's friend very welcome in her house, because this kid can be her eyes to spot predators, supply anxiety management, support, and reassure her son. She needs to participate in and encourage this friendship as much as she can.

"Better to be a first-rate Aspie than a second-rate neurotypical!"

CRAIG: Here's the next question. "My friend has a twenty-five-year-old son with Asperger's. Socially, he has difficulty fitting in with NT peers and this frustrates him. He is angry that he is not normal. Only within the past few years has he begrudgingly acknowledged his diagnosis. Now, knowing this, he also adamantly refuses to associate with other people on the spectrum. He finds himself isolated and lonely, which only makes him angrier. He is not open to discussion about it. What might you suggest for my friend and his son?"

DR. TONY: He's trying to be a second-rate neurotypical when he should be a first-rate Aspie! Many teenagers with Asperger's desperately want to be like everyone else, and will have no tolerance of the word "Asperger's." With maturity, he may start to notice that he does have some differences—but I want him to start looking at his qualities, not his defects.

Sometimes it helps to have a mentor with Asperger's that he values. He's twenty-five, so somebody in their fifties who is a hero to him (is involved in his area of interest, career, etc.) is more believable than somebody in their patronizing way saying, "Just be yourself."

He's isolated and lonely, he needs to meet more Aspies and recognize that. I'd like to explore what his concept of Asperger's is; who has explained it to him? What does he think it is? Then, go through the qualities that make Aspie heroes to him. He needs a paradigm shift to see Asperger's not as a disaster that makes you second-rate, defective, or disturbed, but that it makes you a distinct individual with particular qualities.

By better understanding himself, he'll be better able to explain himself, make friends, and make better career options that are suited to his strengths. He really needs someone to work with him outside the family; perhaps a counselor may be able to do that, but I would like him to have a mentor with Asperger's syndrome who's been through it and has credibility.

CRAIG: Dr. T., is there a book out there about Aspie heroes?

DR. TONY: Yes, there are quite a few, some published by Jessica Kingsley Publishers and Future Horizons. It's beneficial to look at famous scientists, artists, etc., and recognize that by the world values their alternative way of thinking and creating. It's seeing themselves as an advantage to society, not a disadvantage.

"How can I differentiate different levels of friendship?"

CRAIG: Okay, next question. "This person, diagnosed with Asperger's, has always had a hard time making and keeping friends. In his own words, he always ends up pushing them away and smothering them. He would like to learn how to differentiate between all the different levels of friendship such as an acquaintance, a work friend, or a casual friend."

DR. TONY: From my clinical experience, a person with Asperger's has one of three ways of coping with social confusion and social inclusion. There's one group who become very shy, introverted, and don't want to engage. The second group are too intense and intrusive; they annoy people because they just go in and take over what's going on, they can't read other people or see that other people are bored or have other things to do. In their desperation or intention to interact, they are clumsy in that interaction and annoy others. That intensity and inclusiveness may be occurring here. The third option is often used by girls and women, and is much more creative. It is to observe, absorb, and imitate what's going on from a distance before making the first move.

For this individual we would use what we call the "concept of the circle of friends."

Take a big piece of paper and draw a series of concentric circles on it, like a dart board. In the middle is the individual, next maybe parents, in the next circle maybe neighbors—going outward, various people are put on different levels. With this visual, you then go through separate pieces of paper with topics of conversation, appropriate touch, greetings, and so on, so they can understand. Certain circles sometimes have the concentric circles color-coded like a rainbow, with red in the middle and all the colors going outward.

If, for example, somebody is in the green circle, these are the things you can talk about in conversation, these are things that you can do for touch, here's whether or not you two talk about your special

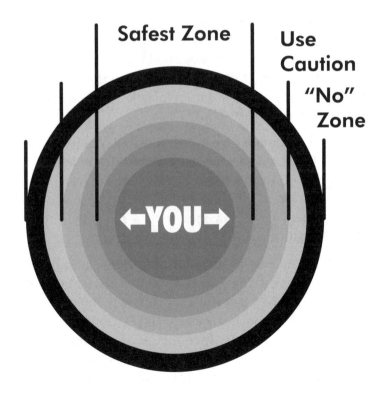

interests. This will help an ASD individual learn the hierarchy of relationships and where people are in their circle; he needs guidance on that. He may also need an opportunity to have these conversations videotaped and to see how he is received by other people. Focus then on what he did right, but then you can replay it, freeze it, and show him what he may have missed.

"How can I work with a group of people?"

CRAIG: This is a question from a math student. "Dear Professor Attwood, I'm a twenty-year-old university math student who is struggling to figure out group work. I'm trying to suppress my controlling nature, but by doing this, it's caused me to be very anxious and worried about the group project all the time. I recently had a public meltdown in front of my group. They don't know about my autism. How can I be a good group member, but also be less anxious about the work? What should I do?"

DR. TONY: An important note for me is that they don't know about your autism. I'm afraid they do need to know. You have a choice: you can use the "A" word and say, "I have autism," which means, "I have a different way of thinking, perceiving, relating, and learning." Interestingly, many famous mathematicians have characteristics of ASD. What is mathematics? It's the study of patterns.

People with autism have been studying patterns all their lives, including social patterns. It means that you may have a mathematical, but not social mindset. They're very different skills. I think that your group needs to know of your diagnosis. Define that and then say, "Guys, I need your help. I tend to be controlling. I'm bossy. I tend to expect others to follow my directions. This is something which I've tried to change, but can you point out when I'm doing it, and give me advice and feedback when I am flexible, cooperative, sharing, and engaging?"

I also think that you need a bit of guidance in social skills. I would hope that the university would have guidance for students with Asperger's on group projects and the things that they're going to need to know. It is the art of compromise, negotiation, and complements. Those are aspects needed to learn in a group setting because that's going to determine whether you get a job or not. Often, for the mathematics students, the biggest problem is not the math, it's group projects. [laughs] I think you're very brave to be trying to do that on your own, but I think you need to let people know about your diagnosis.

Chapter Eight

Personal Management Issues

Chapter Eight — Personal Management Issues

"Would it make more sense for a child to go to school locally and live at home?"

CRAIG: This person has a seventeen-year-old son that is now looking at college, and like most Asperger's students, he has been well provided for with assistance not only in school but at home. This question strikes all of us as parents. "Do we want to send our child away? Would it make more sense for a child to go to school locally and live at home? How should parents approach the discussion and the decision involved when sending a child to college?"

DR. TONY: Usually, people with Asperger's syndrome are still developmentally young in terms of their social and emotional maturity. Although technically he's seventeen years old, he still needs a lot of reassurance and guidance in planning and organizing his day, his school work, and so on. The transition from home to college is an enormous one. Generally, when parents ask me this question, my preference is for the person to live at home if they can. This is for a variety of reasons. Not only do they need help in terms of organizing, planning, time management, and project deadlines, they also need someone to give them a certain sense of reassurance that they're doing well and to help them cope with the issues of potential anxiety, new situations, and making friends.

All these issues in addition to a totally new environment are usually too much at one time. Go to college, yes, but still stay home— don't do both at the same time. It also means that there are issues of their naivety; there's a chance of sexuality, alcohol, drugs, and the individual being taken advantage of. I must admit I've seen many individuals who have collapsed at the end of the first year because of a lack of supervision. I usually advise the student to stay at home if possible. Two very good books that I would recommend are called *Succeeding in College with Asperger's Syndrome* by John Harpur (Jessica Kingsley Publishers) and *Students with Asperger Syndrome: A Guide for College Personnel*. It's by

Lorraine Wolf, with a publication from Autism Asperger Publishing Company.

> **"For some Aspies in high school, consider 'pruning the curriculum.'"**

CRAIG: This next woman writes, "My daughter is sixteen and has Asperger's syndrome. Most colleges want kids to learn a foreign language in high school. Is it harder for an AS kid to learn to use foreign language out of context?"

DR. TONY: Those with autism and Asperger's tend to be at the extremes of ability, whether it be mathematics, spelling, or languages. They're either wonderful at it or hopeless at it. On the one hand, I have those with Asperger's who are multilingual and have an ability to understand language that is intuitive and remarkable. Yet there are others who are hopeless at it. What I look at in high school is what I call "pruning the curriculum."

In other words, if they're not good at it, cut it. There's no point in pursuing it. If she's not good at it or naturally doesn't like it, don't do it.

Chapter Eight — Personal Management Issues

> **"ASD, borderline personality disorder, bipolar, and PTSD. Can I get a clear diagnosis?"**

CRAIG: "I have post-traumatic stress disorder and I get depressed at times. Several people have suggested I may have a type of bipolar or borderline personality disorder on top of my ASD. What would that look like in a person with ASD? Whereas I enjoy solitude and find social situations exhausting, the women I know with BPD are very engrossed in an emotional world that focuses around people and relationships, and they have an overwhelming fear of abandonment. I can see where, superficially, some of the symptoms of BPD and ASD may appear similar, but the significance of these behaviors are really very different. How would I go about getting a clear diagnosis?"

DR. TONY: I see a number of women diagnosed or misdiagnosed with borderline personality disorder. They're not mutually exclusive. In borderline personality disorder, there can be an overreaction to an error: something emotional that occurs in an interpersonal basis, followed by an intense depression attack ("I'm going to kill myself, I'm going to slit my wrists,"). They're called rage attacks. The same can occur with a depression attack, the person with Asperger's may catastrophize an event.

It's part of the problem in emotion regulation where that negative emotion causes a catastrophic overreaction that the person finds difficult to control. Now, one of the characteristics of borderline personality disorder is that the person is assumed to be (and can be) very good at reading facial expressions and body language, and then misinterprets people's intentions. Generally, it is thought that people with ASD are not very good at reading body language. I will challenge that, because my personal experience, clinically and in autobiographies, is that some people with Asperger's have a sixth sense for sensing negative atmosphere.

They're not doing it by facial expressions, they're not doing it by a ton of words, but they just feel that something is wrong. They may use a sixth sense—another channel—to determine negative affect or negative emotions, and then react accordingly. Certainly, there can be strong fears of rejection and abandonment in Asperger's. When their friendships end, they often say, "My friend was disloyal. I was a good friend, why did they abandon me and go to someone else?"

There can be a history of that occurring with a person with Asperger's, and you're dealing here often with women, who will react in a different way than men. Borderline personality disorder can occur in those with autism spectrum disorders, especially the women.

"Asperger's and bipolar. Can they occur together?"

CRAIG: "Do you have any general information on the co-occurrence of Asperger's syndrome or autism in general along with bipolar disorder?"

DR. TONY: There is research on this that was originally conducted way back in the 1970s. It was discovered that, when looking at the parents of a child with autism and Asperger's syndrome, they have a higher-than-expected level of mood disorders. That can include anxiety and depression, but also bipolar (mood fluctuations). When I look at someone with autism and Asperger's syndrome, one of the core features is a difficulty with the perception, understanding, regulation, and management of emotions. This means that the person is very prone to intense emotions. In fact, sometimes the social withdrawal is due to being oversensitive to emotional atmosphere and wanting to avoid situations that appear quite toxic to that individual.

Chapter Eight — Personal Management Issues

This means that with the emotional variability of the day, the person is likely to have stronger reactions than others. When we say bipolar, traditionally it's a change in emotions from depression to euphoria over a matter of weeks or months—a long period of time. Usually with ASD, it's within an hour that the person lurches from one intense emotion to the other. The difficulty there is that emotional range intensity can be very difficult to cope with, both for the person with ASD and others. Whether you can call it bipolar, I'm not too sure.

There's a problem with emotion regulation, and I do ask both the parents and those who have Asperger's to have keep a "mood diary." At the end of the day, determine what your mood has been like. Use a score of zero to twenty, ten for an average day.

At the end of each day, you have a number and you plot that over time. Clearly, there are going to be some extremes. Overall, there may be an unknown cycle. That's very valuable information and

allows you to tell people, "I will be emotionally sensitive and volatile for the next day or two. Please help me."

CRAIG: That brings up the question, do you medicate for bipolar in those with Asperger's syndrome?

DR. TONY: For adults with bipolar, the traditional medication has been lithium, which may not be the first drug of choice for those with autism and Asperger's syndrome. I would normally prefer cognitive behavior therapy because it doesn't have any side effects and teaches the person to use their intelligence to control their emotions. You've got to have a certain degree of maturity and insight, and a developmental level of at least eight or nine to use those strategies. If the person is developmentally younger, or the emotions are very intense, medication may help but that requires a clinician to really know that nature of autism, disentangle what the emotions are, and then prescribe precisely for the emotional problem.

There is a common question that I receive when talking with parents and people with autism and Asperger's: "How do I manage my emotions?"

CRAIG: Yes. Your first solution is to try to do it using your own intellect and ability rather than a medication.

DR. TONY: Also, many of the emotions are a reaction to the environment and sometimes, rather than medication, there may be environmental change and attitude change. That can make a huge difference to the person with Asperger's syndrome. Another factor is to be understood and for other people to be able to read their symptoms. Often the person with Asperger's is the last to know when they're heading into a strong emotion. Others may be able to pick it up sooner, and they need to look at strategies to help.

Chapter Eight — Personal Management Issues

> *"Is bed-wetting common in Asperger's and autism?"*

CRAIG: Here's the next question, Dr. Tony. "I have three Asperger's kids aged seven to nine, and all three visit a regular school and communicate. They're not hyperactive, they're quite intelligent. All three suffer from bed-wetting. Is this common in Asperger's and autism?"

DR. TONY: Yes, it is quite common, and we have several things to look at here. In the typical population, we look at things like anxiety. While that may be a factor in ASD, there's another two components we look at. One is sensory sensitivity, or should I say, the lack of sensitivity. Usually we associate this with touch sensitivity, but there could be a lack of sensitivity to pain and discomfort, causing toileting accidents to occur. This can occur in the day or at night. In other words, the brain is not picking up the signals that they "need to go" until it's too late.

Another component regarding ASD is an altered sleep profile. We're now identifying that sleep profile can be picked up in infants, and it's one of the things we look for early diagnosis. There is a pattern of deep sleep where the brain is switched off and automatic functions occur. So, I would first check on the sensory issue. Is that person less sensitive to pain and discomfort? If so, they're not getting the signals. You need to have an alarm clock go off in the night to alert them to go to the toilet, because the signals aren't getting through. The other option is to have a look at a sleep clinic to see if there's anything that's happening in their sleep cycle that may be affecting them. It's a very serious problem, luckily, most get over it and it's not necessarily lifelong.

CRAIG: Interesting. It is common. For those of you out there that are suffering this issue, it's part of what you find with autism.

Ask Dr. Tony

"What is the correlation between Asperger's and eating disorders?"

CRAIG: "What is the correlation between Asperger's and eating disorders?"

DR. TONY: Again, quite common. Eating disorders occur for a variety of reasons. One is sensory sensitivity. Food is a sensory explosion of aroma, taste, texture, liquidity, and noise. Sometimes there's an aversion for food because the sensory experiences have been so abhorrent, and that individual doesn't want to try anything that could give them that horrible sensation again. So, the person tends to have a restricted diet. Their lunchboxes always carry the same food.

In the teenage years, you can get what I call "Asperger's faulty logic." For example, I met a young woman who has anorexia nervosa. When she was at school, she found that when she'd skipped lunch and had that slightly uncomfortable feeling of being hungry, she had better concentration. She thought, "If I have less food, I'll be able to better concentrate on school work." Another possibility can be that food, because of the sensory sensitivity, becomes a major feature of that person's life—it eventually becomes a special interest. The person may develop a special interest in calories, their weight, numbers, or control. In other words, they develop an experiment about weight using their own body. Anorexia nervosa does occur, but the origins could be very different.

Chapter Eight — Personal Management Issues

"Some stimming might actually be Tourette's, OCD, or anxiety."

CRAIG: The next question is, "My son has been diagnosed with severe autism since the age of two, and he's now sixteen. He stims a lot and given his six-foot-two, 260-pound frame, it's socially inappropriate. His stimming consists of running through the house, hitting the walls and countertops with his fists and the backs of his hands, jumping up and slamming back down with all his might on the floor, and then making loud barking noises similar to what somebody might make if they have Tourette's syndrome. My question is, is there a medication that could possibly calm him? The ones that we've tried don't seem to work. He also has an excellent behavior analyst who's well trained and knowledgeable, but if our son is not calm enough to work, she doesn't seem to be very successful with him. Do you have any suggestions?"

DR. TONY: Yes. You use the term "stim." When I hear the word "stim" I go, "Oooh." There's a lot more to it than just a self-stimulatory behavior. First of all, the person has suggested a distinct possibility (which is Tourette's disorder), and from the description, it could be a Tourette-like characteristic. In this case, the person may benefit from access to expertise on Tourette's syndrome; it has its own sort of medication that may help those sort of tics and mannerisms.

Some stims are Tourette-like tics, but there's another dimension here, and that is routine. He has developed a routine for when he comes in the house, and he's got to complete the sequence. It could well be that this is partially related to emotion management and high levels of anxiety. As many people that have mild anxiety know, routines are soothing and will help. Also, physical activity is a broad way of burning up energy, so it may have value.

It's a sequence or a compulsion that he's got to do as part of an OCD (obsessive compulsive) component, but he's also physically releasing energy. My approach would to look at this as a sign of high-level anxiety. If that's the case, we need to be looking at a new routine

when he comes home that involves a physical activity but isn't so worrying or potentially destructive. He needs a personal trainer to create a new sequence of physical activities he can do.

Find the first trigger, it can even be walking through the door that begins the process. If you have a side door you can establish a new entry—a new starting point—without the expectations of that sequence. If you're going to use medication, it should be primarily to focus on anxiety and obsessive-compulsive disorder rather than sedation.

Now, he's currently taking an antipsychotic; that's basically a sedative. He's obviously had a huge range of medications, but I would recommend somebody focusing specifically on medication for anxiety. As he has a behavior analyst, we should be looking at behaviors that have developed to moderate and express anxiety. Look at the range of different strategies he can use to reduce his anxiety. This one works, but it's upsetting for other people.

What we're trying to do is substitute other things that you can do: get a toolbox of physical activities and relaxing activities to help him calm down or express his anxiety and agitation in a more constructive way. This is not behavior management, this is more cognitive behavior therapy to manage an anxiety-based ritual and routine.

Chapter Eight — Personal Management Issues

> **"Is hoarding a problem that is common to people with autism and Asperger's?"**

CRAIG: The next question for this segment is about hoarding. "Is hoarding a problem that is common to people with autism and Asperger's? I know someone on the spectrum who has a very large collection of things that I would call useless, yet she refuses to get rid of them. I'm not sure whether to take it in stride or to deal with it as a separate issue."

DR. TONY: [laughs] What a lovely question. It is a problem, but it's different from other forms of hoarding. The person with Asperger's finds people very difficult to understand: intrusive, annoying, inconsistent, and they tease you. It's a problem. But objects and interests may be a great delight in life, the person may have greater enjoyment with objects and collections than interpersonal experiences. Also, not only are these objects associated with pleasurable experiences, they define character. They are who you are.

It's similar to the way people will look at photographs to bring back memories of enjoyable moments. Going back to their collection is a way of bringing back the memory of when they found it and saw it. It has many functions, asking the person to throw it away is saying to somebody, "I want to throw out all your old photographs." People would object to that very strongly, but you must be practical and what you may say is, "Perhaps you could try culling a bit of it. How much of it is absolutely needed?"

I know people with Asperger's who have full shipping containers in their backyard. In fact, when we had the floods in Brisbane, the flood took away their containers and all of their possessions. Their devastation was not the financial loss—it was basically their whole life history that had gone in that container.

I think in this sort of situation, balance is necessary. You can say, "Yes. I will recognize it's important to you that you have these, but in practical terms it's taking up space, it's a fire hazard, and people can trip over it. We need to catalogue it, place it, and put it in an environment that you know is perfectly safe so that you've got a safe passage through your house rather than things that are going to fall on you."

"Computers and break rooms for a safe recess?"

CRAIG: The next question comes from Australia. It says, "Hi Dr. Tony, I'm a special needs support teacher at a school in Australia. We have a large cohort of students with ASD. Over the past few years, we set up a room that students can access at break times if they so choose. There's a growing concern in our school that children are accessing the room every break time and they're playing on the computers for each break. There are calls for the room to be timetabled for kids. My gut tells me to fight this because what I see are kids who feel safe, who are making friends (albeit through a common interest in a computer game), and most of the kids will sit with others and take turns to play. I see this as an achievement rather than a concern, but I'd like to get some feedback and some thoughts from you in this matter."

DR. TONY: You're absolutely right. The playground for other kids is a noisy, chaotic, sociable, unstructured, unsupervised heaven where they can run around and socialize and chat. It is hellish for ASD kids for every one of those reasons. Also, in that environment are the bullies. What they've got is a safe sanctuary. The point of having break time is it should be your recess, a break. It should be relaxing and enjoyable.

As far as these guys are concerned, what's enjoyable is being on a computer. As long as they're playing appropriate games and activities, and if they're interacting with each other, it's beneficial; whatever calms them down and lowers their heart rate. If they like being there, they should be there. It's like being in a life raft with sharks all around, and the teachers who want to get rid of this life raft are saying, "Out of the boat, in to the water now. Don't worry, you'll survive, you will enjoy being eaten by sharks."

CRAIG: I love your analogy! I think it's your British accent makes it a bit more interesting, too.

> *"How do we, as parents, educate the educators on autism?"*

CRAIG: "How can we educate educators that autism is not something they can remove from the fabric of a child?"

DR. TONY: I would like for that educator to imagine having autism for a day and to go through the experiences, from sensory sensitivity right through to being bullied and teased. Some educators get it, and sometimes they are very emphatic individuals that really do understand ASD. The trouble is that those who don't get it actually make the life of a person with ASD far worse because they feel that their teacher doesn't understand them.

Then other kids get a green light to torment and tease, because the teacher does not fully understand. If there's anything we can do, it is to educate in terms of courses and material. Some will get it, but some will fall on deaf ears. We really must try to avoid such individuals and carefully select teachers at all levels to make sure they create an ASD-friendly environment.

Ask Dr. Tony

"Mainstream education and autism. Can it work?"

CRAIG: "Will mainstream schools ever work for our special kids?"

DR. TONY: For some yes, for others it's a disaster. If I were designing the worst environment for ASD kids to learn, it would be a classroom with lots of noisy, chaotic, socializing kids, a curriculum that really is not presented in their learning style, and the inability to get away from it all. For some it's hell, for others it is successful. Usually, because they've got a fairly accommodating personality, they will tolerate situations rather than react against it or internalize it. They need good teachers who understand autism, a peer group that supports them, flexibility in the curriculum, and support from the teacher. Yes, it can work, but the resources put into it are usually beyond what is available for those schools.

"Dr. T., what more would you say if ..."

CRAIG: This next question, Dr. T., is for you. "What would you have liked to have added or written differently in your book *The Complete Guide to Asperger's Syndrome*? Two things that stand out to me: the first is black and white and isn't emphasized enough. For example, some people keep a special interest very private and personal. Personally, I don't go on about them and never have, unless someone shows an interest—then they get the dissertation.

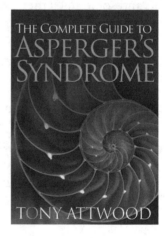

THE COMPLETE GUIDE TO
ASPERGER'S
SYNDROME

TONY ATTWOOD

Chapter Eight — Personal Management Issues

The other is, people with Asperger's syndrome in childhood may outgrow it in adulthood."

DR. TONY: What would I add to the book? One day, hopefully, I will write another. I would include more on sleep issues because I'm finding that is a major problem, and more on sexuality; we had the question about gender identity, but also about intimacy and relationships. I'd also explore more on the sense of self (the question, "Who am I?") and self-acceptance. Also, the aging process and Asperger's syndrome: how do the signs change over time in the last decade of life? I think that would be an important area to focus on.

Now to the original question. For some people with a special interest, it can be very private and personal. What this person has described is that they've acquired the ability to determine whether to talk or not—that's great! He is able to appreciate the perspective of others, and so "compensate" for the Aspie features.

I would also add to the book that about 15 percent of those who have a diagnosis in childhood move into what I call the "subclinical level." This is, if I can indulge for a moment on a particular expression, why the British have understood Asperger's syndrome more than any other nation: because it explains many British characteristics. It explains train-spotters, Oxford and Cambridge University, and the British aristocracy. In any other country, if you collect and display toilet brushes through the ages, you're referred for psychoanalysis for being anally eccentric, whereas the British make a documentary about you with the BBC and you appear on *Antiques Roadshow*. Many people ask, "What's the ultimate Aspie successful outcome?" They become British!

Ask Dr. Tony

"I forget to swallow! And is thumb sucking common with Aspies?"

CRAIG: The next question has two parts. "While I'm focusing on other stuff I forget to swallow, and I get quite a build up to the point that someone has to remind me to. More rarely, the opposite happens and I suddenly noticed that my mouth is quite dry—as if I'd forgotten somehow to produce saliva. That's the first question, is this common? The second is, some people continue thumb-sucking into late stage, either quitting late or never quitting. Are either of these distinct behaviors common with Aspies?"

DR. TONY: I'll take the first one there. People with Asperger's tend to have a one-track mind. They are hyper focused but it's at the cost of other, broader abilities (and that can include toilet training for some). You realize, especially when they're kids, that they've had an accident because they were so involved. Sometimes you need an alarm to go off every so often to indicate needing to go to the restroom, to swallow, etc. That hyper focus is great for work, but a problem if you need to multitask.

Thumb-sucking is present with Asperger's if you have high levels of anxiety; you will do things that are soothing, it's a natural human characteristic. That may be thumb-sucking, tweaking your hair, fiddling with something like rosary beads ... any relaxing, soothing, repetitive behavior. Thumb-sucking is associated with children, so often the task is finding an acceptable substitute.

"Asperger's, parasomnias, and poor sleep patterns."

CRAIG: The next question is from Autism Hangout. "My thirteen-year-old son with Asperger's doesn't sleep much, about three to four hours a night, and the sleep that he does get is disturbed by what his doctors called 'parasomnias.'"

DR. TONY: Parasomnias, yes.

CRAIG: "They have diagnosed him with sleep disorder. We've tried Melatonin, having his sleep hygiene totally by the book, we've looked at his diet, and he has kept a journal to try and dump his thoughts into. He has exercised and he even has quiet downtime. His EEGs have come back clear from epilepsy and we have tried just about everything we can barring prescription sleeping medications. He wakes up tired in the morning from all the shouting and fighting. Dr. Tony, is there any hope that my son will actually get a full night's restful sleep?"

DR. TONY: He needs it, we all need it. There's a very good book which I'm going to recommend from Jessica Kingsley Publishers, it's called *Sleep Difficulties and Autism Spectrum Disorders—A Guide for Parents and Professionals* by Kenneth Aitken.

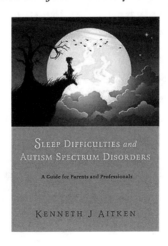

We sleep because we need physical rest. We need sleep to lay down memory traces of long-term memory, consolidating important information from that day throughout the neural structure of the brain. Throughout the day we have an emotional mind, like a whiteboard, and the emotions have been written on the day in various colored markers. As you sleep it's wiped clean, which means a lot of dreams are negative emotions that you're washing out of your system—especially anxiety.

Those with ASD are notoriously poor sleepers, it's constitutional. It should almost be in the diagnostic criteria. What tends to occur is that they may not get the type of sleep where you dream (REM sleep), which is when you do the emotional cleansing of the system. Hence, he's going to have high levels of anxiety, agitation, and so on.

Normally we would refer the person to a sleep clinic, but it seems that this person has already been referred to one.

We have sleep "switches" and one of them is serotonin. We know that there can be serotonin dysfunction in those with autism spectrum disorders. The difficulty is that prescription sleeping medication knocks you out but doesn't do the emotional cleansing. It's great if you need to sleep because you are on an aircraft, for example, and you just want to pass the time, but it doesn't really sort everything out. It doesn't give you constructive sleep. You're just out of it.

I wish I could answer that and I know research is being done on this. All I can ask is that you scan the Internet to see if you can find anything, and read the book. Your son needs a lot of compassion and you need to talk to experts. If necessary, go to your local university and say, "Who's doing research in sleep? My thirteen-year-old son would make an excellent study; looking at EEG sleep architecture, he complicates all these established theories when he is asleep. You may discover some wonderful things about sleep through my son, please examine him."

CRAIG: We can just be hopeful.

DR. TONY: Yes, I'm afraid so.

"Difficulty managing emotions."

CRAIG: "I'm the mother of a five-year-old boy with Asperger's. My son gets angry and frustrated easily and has trouble with emotional management. If a teacher asks him to write, he interprets it as, 'The teacher's mean, she makes us work hard.' If we ask him to hurry up and get ready for school he interprets it as, 'You tell me to do everything, you think you are my boss.' This can lead to a tantrum. I understand cognitive behavior therapy can help resolve this, but he may be too young for that. Please let me know if you have any advice."

DR. TONY: I wouldn't recommend CBT. I'd recommend Carol Gray's *Social Stories™ in Comic Strip Conversations.* *Social Stories™* will explain why the teacher asks him to do things that are difficult: to make him more intelligent and more successful. These are comic strip conversations where you draw the situation with stick figures and speech and thought bubbles. He can write what he thinks the teacher is thinking in the thought bubble and you can go through

it with him and say, "Actually, let's find out what she was really thinking." Then you write in, "I was actually thinking _____," which makes the world more logical.

I would use *Social Stories*™ to explain the logic of why he's being asked to do things and give him insight into the thoughts and feelings of others. He's projecting motives onto others, but he doesn't know how to read the real motives.

"Too much imaginative, internal play! Can we change this behavior?"

CRAIG: "I'm writing regarding a significant challenge for our nine-year-old son, who's diagnosed with Asperger's. The concern is internal, scripted, and extended imagined play that presents itself in two ways. First as inattention when faced with independently completing a multi-step task (such as getting ready in the morning), and second as social disengagement when playing on the playground during recess.

"To address the issue of completing multi-step tasks, we have tried multiple strategies with limited success. We've tried checklists, timers, and rewards. To address the impact on participation in social settings, I've worked with the school; however, he's expressed a strong preference for continuing with his imaginative play. We have thought that his behavior may be a means of managing anxiety. What is the best way to address these behaviors?"

DR. TONY: Well, he's probably enjoying his imaginative play as one of the greatest experiences in his life. One thing that those with Asperger's are very good at is using their imagination. Another thing they're very good at is worrying. Their imagination can be a wonderful way of coping, they can escape into the world where they're successful and their intelligence is appreciated.

It's also an escape mechanism when overwhelmed or confused. In a playground there may be too much going on, but if he is escaping through his imagination, he's safe. It also acts as a thought blocker. If he's anxious, he can escape the reality of the situation. It has many functions for him. As he's nine years old, he doesn't yet have the cognitive maturity to stop it. I'm afraid an external voice, an adult, needs to remind him gently to get back to the task at hand.

It's really something that he has in his character. Psychologically, it's a good coping mechanism, it's a wonderful one. The problem is that it's so enjoyable and so effective he finds it very difficult to switch off. It can only be switched off by an adult. Don't get upset with him, but just call his name and say, "You need to get back on task." This does seem to suggest that he is overwhelmed in some situations.

Is he anxious about his school performance? Why is he needing to switch off and escape into his imagination? I would explore it further because it's his way of saying, "I'm finding this situation very difficult to cope with."

> **"Regression in toilet training. It's hurting her socially."**

CRAIG: "A seven-year-old Aspie girl who was toilet trained seems to have regressed and is now toileting outside. She's doing number twos like a dog would, just as she's going to school and walking across the lawn. She's been having problems at her school as the school teachers just do not seem to understand nor care about her. Her parents have been doing all they can to help, but the school seems to be holding her back. She's constantly left out of social situations and she's picked on by other kids. She is a very social girl but has no real understanding of social situations. Can you offer some positive and constructive advice?"

DR. TONY: Wow. I seriously wonder, as she's a seven-year-old Aspie girl, if she's actually pretending to be a dog and going to the toilet like one because dogs are friendly—unlike other kids. Dogs are

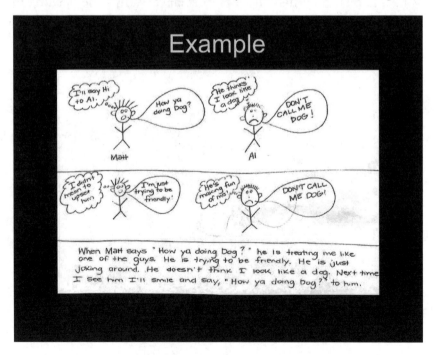

pleased to see her, they're non-judgmental, they're kind, incredibly supportive, and tolerant. Dogs seem to fit much better in this person's life than actual people. So, I wonder, with her seven-year-old mentality, if she would like to be a dog because dogs are good? It seems that she is very social, but constantly left out of situations.

The solution is to find one or two kids that can adopt, support, include, and value her for who she is. I'm very concerned that when she's picked on, she's likely to absorb what they say. Later on, I look at teenagers and some of their defensive issues and I ask them, "What thoughts go through your mind when you're feeling so sad?" They tell me their thoughts and I think, "Wow, your parents never told you that, you've gotten that from other kids. In other words, you started to believe them, and those seeds have borne fruit later on." It's very important that the peer group is supportive to her, and I think she's just finding a way of escaping from the situation: her imagination.

I would use *Social Stories*™ by Carol Gray, where you draw stick figures with speech bubbles and thought bubbles. Draw one where she is walking on the lawn and she goes number two, then write in what she's thinking, how she's feeling, and how other people are reacting to her (in a non-judgmental way).

We need to find out what's going on in her mind, but I think she may be escaping into becoming an animal because it's safer and animals are nice to her when people aren't.

Ask Dr. Tony

CRAIG: This next question also has to do with accepting ASD behaviors. In this case, it's motor mannerisms. "Our son, who is sixteen and high-functioning, has been working through his motor mannerisms issue with an excellent psychologist. Unfortunately, they don't seem to be making any progress. I'd really like some advice as to where to go next, as this is a big problem for him socially. Thank you in advance."

DR. TONY: Again, an interesting question. There are many reasons for motor mannerisms. First, they're an expression of a thought or emotion. There's a happiness flap or a little excitement jiggle that expresses emotions in an unusual but endearing way. I always say, "The mannerisms have a message." A mannerism can express what he's thinking or feeling, and that's useful information. Another reason would be that they're Tourette-like tics, and these are involuntary actions. When you have these, the problem is that they are subconscious actions. Behavioral approaches of rewards and consequences won't work because the person is not thinking before they do them. They just happen.

If he's sixteen, it is quite possible that within the next two or three years these could disappear almost completely. However, if they're involuntary mannerisms, it's going to be very difficult for him to inhibit them. He may suppress them for awhile but behind closed doors, he may engage in those mannerisms. That creates so much stress.

Again, I would use the approach of explaining what he has to the people that know him: "I have these little mannerisms. They're just something I do all of a sudden. They're not significant, let's carry on with the conversation."

Chapter Eight — Personal Management Issues

"Who is a good person, and who is bad? How to tell?"

CRAIG: This next question has to do with teaching how to recognize good people from bad people. "Dear Dr. Attwood, I have a friend who has a nine-year-old son who's Aspie. He will do anything anyone asks of him, regardless of the consequences. Mom cannot, despite her best efforts, get him to understand that there are people in the world who will have malevolent intentions toward him. What can his mom do to be successful in giving him the gullibility talk before he has to learn that lesson the hard way?"

DR. TONY: Two things here. One, he needs a guardian amongst his peer group, someone who is streetwise, nine years old, and is going to grow up to be a good guy. They need to be briefed that your son is vulnerable, gullible, and delightful, but he's an easy target. Say to the one or two kids, "You are good at spotting the predators, you know who they are. They're like sharks circling a victim; when you see them circling, please step in and say, 'Hi,' or stand next to him so that you can listen to what they're saying."

Tell your son that sometimes, this guardian/friend will want to be with him just to check if he's talking to good guys or not. With a nine-year-old, I would describe personalities as animals. I'd ask him, "If you were an animal, what would you be?" For many folks with Asperger's, it's either a bird or a dog ... those are common ones. Then you can ask questions like, "Who do you know that would be a friendly dog? Who do you know that is a cat, they want to be with you but they tend to wander off? Who do you know that would be a snake or a spider, and could be dangerous? Who do you know that could be a wolf in sheep's clothing?" Go through animals as a metaphor for personality.

I would go through a range of words that describe personality types. With young children, you can always use acting activities. Ask, "What can be the signs someone is asking you to do something that might be not so good?" Then, rehearse what to say. "Are you being friendly or not friendly? I want to check that out first. I'm not sure." "If you have any thoughts that this may be something you feel uncomfortable about, check it out with someone else. That's a smart thing to do."

Chapter Nine

Intimacy, Dating, Sex, Marriage, and Emotional Availability

Chapter Nine — Intimacy, Dating, Sex, Marriage, and Emotional Availability

"I have no understanding of flirtation or non-verbal sexual cues ... and I've been taken advantage of."

CRAIG: This next question is a little disturbing, but it's not the first time this situation has occurred. This was written in Autism Hangout, "I'm an Aspie teen and I may have a fully developed female body, but I have no understanding of flirtation or non-verbal sexual cues."

This woman feels that she has been susceptible not only to harassment, but even date rape. She says, "I have, on numerous occasions, been taken sexual advantage of and I find myself touching myself excessively. Is that normal for an Aspie to do after being sexually assaulted? If it is, how can I stop this?" She also wants to know if she can learn other non-verbal sexual cues that will help her in the future.

DR. TONY: This is a very worrying situation, and I have a few thoughts on this. The "dating game" is a very complex activity; usually teenagers go through a group of friends, gradually moving along the continuum of intimacy, from meeting somebody they like right through to a whole range of sexual activities. The person gradually moves along that timeline and a range of activities over a number of years with support from their peers.

Girls in particular tend to go out with other girls, and they have a built-in radar system of good guys and bad guys. There's always friends around to assist in case there's an emergency. If the girl knows someone and feels safe, they may gradually move on to a relationship. For girls with Asperger's syndrome, they often don't have that information. I remember a very powerful comment from Liane Holliday Willey: when she meets someone new, she has a core of neurotypical friends who are good judges of character.

If you meet someone who likes you and you like them, it's recommended that you introduce them to a family member, friend, or someone you trust who can get to know them and give you advice as to whether they are a reputable person or not. What you do in a relationship is a decision between two of you, but it is very important to progress at a rate that you feel comfortable with.

It's important that you go to places where there are lots of other people around and that are relatively safe. When someone has been sexually abused, there will obviously be a very significant effect on that person's psyche which can be expressed in a variety of ways. What the woman mentions is that she may excessively touch herself, and this may be one of the reactions from being sexually assaulted. I do recommend that she talks to someone about her sexual experiences in counseling with someone she trusts.

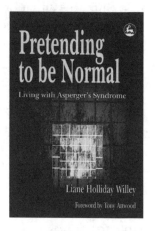

If she does find someone to talk to, they may not know about Asperger's syndrome, in which case they need to read the relevant literature to understand her reaction. Often the person with Asperger's can explain events in a very detached way, which other people find quite odd. The person with Asperger's is giving you information without the emotion, that can be confusing for a neurotypical counselor.

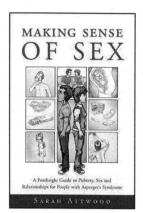

I'm very concerned that she is worried that this will happen again, and she really does need guidance—not only in who would make a good friend, but also aspects of sexuality. I recommend a book written by my wife called *Making Sense of Sex*, it's designed for teenagers with Asperger's to understand aspects of sexuality and relationships. It's published by Jessica Kingsley

Chapter Nine — Intimacy, Dating, Sex, Marriage, and Emotional Availability

publishers and it's titled *A Forthright Guide to Puberty, Sex and Relationships for People with Asperger's Syndrome.*

"Does Asperger's get more exaggerated or more involved with age?"

CRAIG: The next question is regarding Aspie/NT marriages. "Do the behaviors and mindsets of adults with Asperger's increase as they age? Does Asperger's get more exaggerated or more involved with age? As my husband gets older he's withdrawing more, and becoming indifferent to the hurts that he inflicts on our marriage and to our children. In his words, he says he couldn't care less who he hurts."

DR. TONY: Very good question there. When we look at ASD, there is a fluctuation in the signs throughout life. Sometimes the features are very powerful in the preschool years (hyperactive, very intense) but during primary or elementary school years, there can be a degree of stability and progress in a variety of ways. Of course, puberty throws everything up in the air and we have huge changes. In the mid-twenties and onwards comes a greater degree of maturity, a cognitive ability not to get so upset by situations, the ability to read social cues, and an understanding of what's required of them learned by observation, guidance, and support.

Some of the characteristics can diminish over time, but I think this woman may be talking about somebody in their last decade or two of life. What I find tends to occur is that the person with Asperger's wonders, "What's my role? What's my script?" They know what they're expected to do by observing, but to a certain extent in the last of the decades of life, they don't care.

It's a normal human characteristic to be less careful about what you say and what you do. The person is not becoming malicious, they're becoming less concerned about how their behavior affects other people. Those features can increase as the person ages and they become truer to their earlier childhood level. Shakespeare was very good in describing certain ages of man, and this is what you get. So yes, the person can increase their ASD characteristics as they go back through their lifetime.

"How do NT's react when the partner is diagnosed with ASD?"

CRAIG: "What is a common reaction of an NT partner to an AS partner when they are diagnosed?"

DR. TONY: There are number of reactions. One is, "I always thought he would change. I always thought the solution was going to be simple, he would just choose to change, but he hasn't done it yet." Now it's a recognition that maybe he can't, maybe it's a genuine difficulty.

It takes the wind out of your sails, too, because you can get angry. And then you suddenly realize in a compassionate way that he didn't know, rather than he won't do it. There can also be a sense of relief to know that it's not your fault, and that there is an explanation.

Now, the next reaction can be one of, "We know it's Asperger's." First of all, does the Aspie partner agree with the neurotypical's assessment that they're Aspie? The Aspie partner can disagree, and that can lead to major difficulties. If they insist they're not, then they're not going to get on board with the strategies.

For some, the Aspie partner recognizes it in themselves and they can both work together to understand the cultural differences. It's

Chapter Nine — Intimacy, Dating, Sex, Marriage, and Emotional Availability

a marriage of two different cultures, two different priorities, two different perceptions, and the ability to work together constructively. The issue is going to be figuring out how to do that. You'll need external support in a variety of ways. There are some very good books that are written for couples to work through if they can't find a relationship counselor who knows what to do.

Secondly, see if it's possible to find a relationship counselor who knows Asperger's. Otherwise, the relationship counseling probably isn't going to work, because it's based on neurotypical couples and this couple is different.

The third component is the necessity of support groups for the neurotypical. We have one in Brisbane, it's a wonderful organization. We meet on the first Saturday of the month; it's predominantly women, but not exclusively. It's an opportunity to express your experiences with a group of people who genuinely understand. We pass around the tissue box, not for tears of disparities but tears of laughter in discussing their stories! There's a wonderful sense of relief that you're not alone.

We have people in the support groups who are very deeply in love with a person with Asperger's. Some are in the very early stages of the relationship, right through to those who are grandparents. They can support each other as those who have been through those situations and can give advice based on their experiences.

Advice from their personal experience, advice from relationship counselors, and advice from literature. That's what I would suggest for this person.

"I feel like I'm dying inside. Can AS spouses learn, adapt, and relate to their NT spouse in a healthy way?"

CRAIG: "I've been married for twenty-six years to a man I now believe has AS. Although I would like to save the marriage, I cannot live the rest of my life with no emotional understanding or support from him. I feel like I'm dying inside. Can AS spouses learn, adapt, evolve, and relate to their neurotypical spouse in a healthy way?"

DR. TONY: Yes, he undoubtedly can! But there are many components that need to be considered. First of all, the person with Asperger's must recognize the characteristics in themselves. I'm not suggesting that they must go for a formal diagnosis, it's more a question of acknowledging privately within the relationship that the descriptions of Asperger's syndrome apply to their personality and abilities. The first step is realizing, "Yes, this is me, these are the issues I do have in terms of my ability to show the degree of affection you're expecting. I thought it was enough. I feel I've disappointed you in many ways or I may not understand your perspective."

Chapter Nine — Intimacy, Dating, Sex, Marriage, and Emotional Availability

The second is motivation, and sometimes the person with Asperger's may not be aware of the effect on their partner. They may think the relationship is going well, because they're happy. ("I'm okay, so you must be okay.") He may not understand the other person's perception of the difficulties in the relationship. The neurotypical may be looking for more communication, more intimacy, more compassion—there's a whole range of things that are anticipated in a relationship—but the person with Asperger's may not know when it's needed or how to give it.

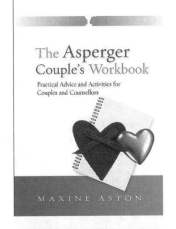

There needs to be a sense of motivation to change. Once that person with Asperger's is motivated, they will change and they will be successful. One thing I've noticed in those with Asperger's is that when they get on board with something, they do it thoroughly and in a very different way. Get them on track and they'll reach the destination, but you've got to get them on track. Also,

once there's motivation, you've got to check the degree of motivation of both parties in the relationship (where they see it going, and so on) and then provide information.

When I do relationship counseling with couples, I'm acting as an advocate and translator for both parties to help them really learn how to relate. There are two excellent books on this, one by Maxine Aston called *The Asperger Couple's Workbook*, the other by Louise Weston titled *Connecting with Your Asperger Partner.* These are written primarily by couples themselves about what they found successful.

There can be progress in the relationship but it requires improving communication and mutual understanding. Usually you'll need a professional who knows how to navigate that area to help, but some relationship counselors don't know about ASD and that can be confusing. If that's the case, I would recommend using the books first. Also, if there's a degree of embarrassment about those issues, then reading the books may be a private way of gaining the information. So yes, it can happen. I can't guarantee it, but you need acceptance of the characteristics, motivation to change, and access to information and support.

"A twenty-two-year-old body with the social maturity of a twelve-year-old."

CRAIG: "Please explain how a twenty-two-year-old adult with Asperger's perceives social and sexual maturity if he has the social maturity of a twelve-year-old."

DR. TONY: Okay. He's twenty-two, he has the physical maturity of a twenty-two-year-old in sexual response (such as an erection) that will have occurred in line with puberty as a natural process. His level of social-emotional maturity is that of a twelve-year-old, and also his knowledge of friendship and relationships will be very young. He needs to learn about friendship rather than dating, and how to meet people. What he would expect here is not "intimacy" but "liking someone." When he likes someone, what could he say? What could he do?

Chapter Nine — Intimacy, Dating, Sex, Marriage, and Emotional Availability

MINDS & HEARTS

07 3844 9466
info@mindsandhearts.net
07 3844 9533

HOME EVENTS ASSESSMENT THERAPY TEAM RESOURCES FEES & REBATES BOOKS THRIVING AT WORK CONTACT

Asperger's Syndrome and Autism Spectrum Conditions:
Training Events and Psychology Services

Events → read more
Children → read more
Teens and Adults → read more

Minds & Hearts provides services and training specifically for Asperger's Syndrome and Autism.

If he gets to know them and likes them, these are some compliments he could say that are appropriate and not embarrassing. As a young man, he may say, "I like your hair," rather than, "I think you've got a great chest," (which really doesn't go over very well to say when dating). He really needs to explore the relationship side beyond friendship. Now, at the Minds and Hearts clinic in Brisbane, we've been going through this in a program called Beyond Friendship which includes the dating game. How do you know when someone likes you? How can you express that to avoid issues like stalking when a simple act of kindness is perceived as more than was really intended?

You have someone who needs to know what girls would like; girls could talk to him about wanting someone who is trustworthy, loyal, and friendly to help him understand. Otherwise, he's going to get the idea of what it's supposed to be like from the media. The media has a certain description which he may not fit, and then feel despondent that he's not like the current heartthrob of the time. "I don't look like Brad Pitt or have Chris Pratt's body. I'll never be successful."

He needs to learn what girls find attractive, what qualities he has, how to meet people, and to first become friends. As he gets to know them, then perhaps he may seek permission: "Would it be okay to hold your hand?" for example. My concern is if he's twenty-two and he's got the social maturity of a twelve-year-old, he may well have Internet access.

If his maturity is that of a twelve-year-old, he may be interested in the bodies of and a relationship with a prepubescent girl. If that's his level of maturity and he is seeking access to images of that on the Internet, he could then be arrested for the possession of child pornography, which could cause considerable difficulties. My advice in this situation is that he needs to understand friendship and the art of flirting rather than intimacy and dating at this stage.

"Past military, PTSD, ASD, and intimacy. Where does one start?"

CRAIG: "Hi, I recently met a guy who was in the army for ten years, has PTSD, and I'm convinced he's an Aspie. He's obsessed with rocks; he rides his bike around all day looking for them, and he smokes cigarettes and drinks lots of energy drinks. One time when we were hanging out, he basically sexually assaulted me and then claimed it was my fault. He intrigues me a lot but he has a lot of problems. I'm concerned is he going through a lot and doesn't know how to handle sexuality. How does the army affect Aspies?"

Well, clearly, there's more in here than just the last question.

DR. TONY: Indeed. Let's start with the last bit; how does the army affect Aspies? The army can be very appealing because it has structure, hierarchy, purpose, and clear rules. In the army, you can be anything from a truck driver to an infantry person or a helicopter

Chapter Nine — Intimacy, Dating, Sex, Marriage, and Emotional Availability

pilot. It's very appealing that it will train you in various careers. That degree of predictability and certainty of role can be very appealing. You have an alternative family, in a way.

This person does seem to have PTSD. As a separate issue, the level of PTSD in Asperger's is very high and I often have to distinguish between the Asperger's and PTSD; maybe not from a war zone, but perhaps from being sexually assaulted, bullied, or teased. All those sorts of things cause great stress.

PTSD and ASD often go together and are a very particular combination with specific needs for therapy. With this person, I don't know what's occurred, but it seems the military may have been traumatizing for him. The person who wrote this is clearly a very compassionate, caring, maternal person who has seen someone that needs to be taken in and looked after.

This is a big problem, and you can't solve it on your own. If he's ex-military, there will be rehabilitation services, and you might encourage him to engage with those services for professionals to deal with the PTSD. If he has Asperger's syndrome, then you may talk to those agencies regarding a need for a diagnosis because it will affect the treatment and support that he's going to need.

Clearly, there are aspects of his life that suggest he could have Asperger's, and he may have issues with intimacy and dating. He needs guidance. Whether the person who wrote this is the person to do that is debatable, and I would say they certainly need help from professional services from the Army as well as friends and relatives. It's a big ask to do that. If he's prepared to do it, good on you. But you need reinforcements to support you.

Ask Dr. Tony

"Difficulties in reading subtle cues, feelings, and thoughts."

CRAIG: "I have high-functioning autism and my partner has been diagnosed with Asperger's syndrome. My partner and I have tried to have a healthy sex life but there are some critical barriers. Though she knows how to initiate sex, she just can't bring herself to do it. She either says, 'I can't do it' or 'I just don't know how.' She has asked me to be more forward with my sexual advances so it will be easier for her to go along with. I find it hard to make clear what I want, I feel like the things I do are sleazy advances. I'm quite embarrassed about it. Are there strategies that we can put in place that would help?"

DR. TONY: When we look at dating, romance, and intimacy, it can be difficult for those with Asperger's to read the deepest and most subtle of thoughts and feelings. There can be performance anxiety: not knowing whether they will do well, whether they will read the signals, whether their performance is going to be good. This goes

for both males and females. That performance anxiety can lead to thoughts like, "I might make a mistake." The important thing here is that anxiety and sex really don't tend to go together. I do strongly recommend that this couple go to a relationship counselor that focuses on aspects of intimacy.

Since both partners in this situation have Asperger's syndrome, by definition they both will have difficulties with communication. I think they need a third party, a relationship counselor, who can work on this. One of the things to discuss is making "sleazy advances." That may be a sort of description of how the person feels. Be open and honest about the situation, and don't be anxious with or embarrassed by the other party. What they need is knowledge from someone who's an expert in this area. There are books specifically written for those with Asperger's on this topic.

> *"So many changes come with pregnancy! I'm frightened of sex and pregnancy."*

CRAIG: "Hello, I am a twenty-eight-year-old Aspie from the Czech Republic. I've always been frightened of sex and pregnancy. I find pregnant women repulsive and I can't even imagine being pregnant one day. I'm frightened that I will look and feel like an unappealing whale and my future husband will lose any interest in me. Everybody keeps saying when I'm ready, I'll love being pregnant and feel beautiful, but I know I won't. My fear is so intense that if I found out I was going to have a baby I would rather have an abortion. I would like to have a child one day, I really like children. I am also afraid that they would never let me adopt a kid because I have Asperger's. The thought of not having children is unbearable and painful to me. Is there a way to get rid of the fear?"

DR. TONY: Thank you for a very interesting question. I think you are right in disagreeing with those telling you that when you're pregnant you will change your way of thinking; I think you will feel unsettled about the whole process. But as a psychologist reading between the lines, what I pick up here is fear of rejection from other people. You're already sensitized to how people may look at your body and tease you about it.

In Asperger's, the person may not be able to easily disclose their thoughts and feelings, but what they use to resolve anxiety is knowledge. Look into the reasons you become larger, how it affects the body, and remember that this is only a temporary component. Find out as much as you can about it, and keep note that the outcome is well worth it because you have a baby. You're only pregnant for nine months and yet you could be a parent for about fifty years. Now, what you may have is a fear of body image acceptance, meaning you may need cognitive behavior therapy from a psychologist to help reduce that fear.

"Platonic or sexual relationships with ASD? How can an NT tell what's going on?"

CRAIG: We have some more relationship questions, they're kind of all lumped together. "Four months ago, I realized my boyfriend has Asperger's syndrome like his brother and his mother. We've been a couple for five years now and at this point, he's met another girl who has ADHD and he hangs out with her. This worries me since I have realized that he has no idea how to interact with women and where the boundaries are.

"They are running together every week and changing clothes in the same room. I've already tried to talk to him, but he says I'm being controlling. How does it work with ADHD and AS? Is the mixture negative? What kind of outlook should I have on this to avoid getting hurt all the time?"

DR. TONY: People with Asperger's syndrome may not know where the boundaries are, what the social conventions are in a relationship, or how what they're doing affects the thoughts and feelings of others. There are three dimensions here. The chances are that the boyfriend is being quite honest and upfront and he's not concerned with gender, he's more concerned with the quality of a person and what they do. Now, the person who's written in this question is obviously sensitive to being hurt. She's projecting various worries onto the situation as though he were a neurotypical. He's an Aspie. There's a 90 percent chance it's platonic, but just watch it because you don't know who the other person is and if you can trust them.

> **"More concern: platonic or sexual relationships with ASD? How can an NT tell what's going on?"**

CRAIG: The next question is similar. "Assuming a person is a special interest, is informed, and doesn't object, should it be discouraged? What if the Aspie's wife is upset that another female is a non-romantic special interest?"

DR. TONY: Oh, that's interesting. When I was doing a relationship session with a group of partners one of the women said, "My husband couldn't have an affair because he can only cope with one person at a time. He couldn't cope with two women." I think the interest can be a person, but it's usually at an intellectual level. As long as the other person realizes that the interest is at an intellectual and platonic level, that should be okay. The person with Asperger's may not understand their partner's feelings in this, and it needs to be explained by a third party.

Otherwise, their reaction is, "You're just trying to stop me from having fun, you're being mean to me," when that's not the intention. The person may not be aware of the concept of jealousy. Temple Grandin said she really doesn't understand the concept of jealousy. Someone in authority, especially someone who knows about ASD, needs to say to this person, "Your wife is concerned for these reasons and they are legitimate. You need to address them."

CRAIG: What might an Aspie do or say to their NT spouse in a situation like this to show that he understands she's jealous?

DR. TONY: I think somebody needs to do a bit of a project on the concept of jealousy, why neurotypicals feel jealous, and the idea that in a relationship you're looking for someone who is trustworthy. What makes a good friend, what makes a good partner? How can you demonstrate this in the relationship?

"It's the intellect I'm interested in ... not a sexual relationship."

CRAIG: We've had a lot of discussions about the difference between special interest friends and intimate friends. From the outside, a neurotypical looking at a relationship between someone with Asperger's and an NT could think it's intimate when it is actually nothing more than a special friendship. One example would be a professor and a student, where the student to some degree looks like he or she is idolizing the professor, but it's a very platonic thing.

Chapter Nine — Intimacy, Dating, Sex, Marriage, and Emotional Availability

DR. TONY: Those with Asperger's may idolize intellect, not physique. [laughs] In other words, they're not necessarily having a "crush" in terms of wanting a sexual relationship, they're just admiring the intellect of that person. The tendency is to assume that people are sexually oriented. Many people with Asperger's are asexual: they're not interested in a sexual relationship with anyone. They're interested in an intellectual relationship and may be very enthusiastic, but people will project onto that person that their motives are sexual.

CRAIG: That frames up a question nicely. This person is wondering how to protect the people involved in a non-romantic, special-interest relationship. Is it in her best interest to say, "This is my sister; she's a student and she's not looking at him in a sexual way, she's admiring his intellect?"

DR. TONY: Absolutely! In Asperger's, intellect can be one of the most important (if not the most important) personality characteristics that you admire in people. In fact, the person with Asperger's is then horrified that people would think they're being sexual when they are really thinking, "I'm interested in his ideas. I'm interested in what he says, because it's so fascinating." The degree of passion for the ideas is assumed to be a sensual, sexual passion, but it's an intellectual passion.

CRAIG: Okay, is that something that we try to explain to other NTs?

DR. TONY: Yes, because otherwise they'll misinterpret. The person who is the focus of the special interest usually recognizes it's not sexual or sensual, because they just sense that it's the mind that's being explored. Other people think, "Oh, with that degree of adulation, there must be a hidden agenda. She's doing this so she can appeal to that person to get higher grades."

CRAIG: Why are we, as NTs, sometimes so disgusting in the conclusions we draw?

DR. TONY: Because we look at ourselves and what we would do in that situation and realize they're completely different motives.

"He ran away in a panic as soon as he asked me to marry him."

CRAIG: Very good. The next question reads, "He ran away in a panic as soon as he asked me to marry him! What can I do to soothe my ASD fiancé?"

DR. TONY: The keyword is panic! There's also uncertainty because he didn't know what the outcome was going to be. He had enormous courage to ask, but then ran away because he wasn't sure of the answer. Use a soothing approach to that individual and find out from them. You can ask, "What are you scared about? What are you anxious about?" Then reassure that person.

Chapter Nine — Intimacy, Dating, Sex, Marriage, and Emotional Availability

"If one parent has AS, what are the odds a kid will have it?"

CRAIG: "I've heard that there's a 90 percent chance that a baby will have an ASD if one of the parents has one. Is this true? If my child turns out to have an ASD as well, I'm not sure I would be able to cope with dealing with two Aspies at the same time. Do you have any thoughts on this?"

DR. TONY: The statistics are wrong. W-R-O-N-G, wrong. Yes, there is a genetic element and we're looking at the genogram for both sides. For some—half the cases we see—the cause of ASD is not genetics. It's something that occurred in utero and affected the brain's development. Both parties may scan their own and their partner's genetic history and not have ASD present.

In half the cases we see, it's not inherited. It may be genetic material, but as a one-off, similar to how Down syndrome isn't inherited. The other component the research is starting to look at is the recurrence rate; if you have one child with Asperger's and you have a subsequent male child, that boy has a 25 percent chance of ASD.

From my own clinical experience with genetics, when the mother has Asperger's she may have a fifty-fifty chance with each conception—which may be a greater level than the father. This has not been confirmed with research, but it's my own clinical opinion. It's not a 90 percent chance, it's much less than that.

The subsequent question she asks is, "How will I cope?" How will you cope when you have kids, whatever the child may be? It's very hard to determine that. You don't know how you're going to cope; you don't know how your partner's going to cope, either. That's a whole other topic: is the person with Asperger's going to have confidence and ability in their parental role? If you do conceive and you do carry that child all the way through, you may not know for sure if they have an ASD until they're over three years old.

That means throughout the pregnancy and for the first three years of life you're going to be so sensitive, thinking, "He looked away. He looked away. Does he have autism? He flinched at that sound, that must be autism." You've got to be careful or you're going to project all sorts of things on that child. All aspects of ASD occur in the ordinary population—what makes them significant is their dominance, not their existence.

How are you going to cope? I don't know. It depends on the child. What I can say categorically is that it is not a 90 percent chance. If you've heard, "When a parent has Asperger's, you can guarantee that that kid is going to be Asperger's," this is not the case at all.

CRAIG: That's very good news.

Chapter Ten

Faking It

Chapter Ten — Faking It

CRAIG: This next question begins, "I'm forty-six, and I diagnosed myself at age forty." He talks about a term he refers to as an "Aspergian mask." He says, "I am so good at pretending to be normal that my now ex-doctor didn't believe I was actually on the spectrum." Here's his question: "I don't like being fake. What can I do to communicate better? How can I learn to have a relationship? How can I live without wearing an 'Aspergian mask?'"

DR. TONY: It's a coping mechanism that starts off when you're young. It's an intelligent way of coping, following thoughts like, "I'm not successful at fitting in. I'm concerned about my emotions, and my emotions put people off. My social confusion and clumsiness puts people off, so I'll create a mask, I'll create a persona. They won't see the emotion behind, they won't see the social confusion." The trouble is, you then suppress parts of yourself, and what you're doing is "faking it." It's an exhausting process, but it works, and sometimes people are so good at it that others can't recognize the amount of intellectual effort that went into it.

There's a feeling of not being able to show the real you, that there's something despicable about you and you've got to keep the act together. But it's making you depressed. The question is, should you take that mask off? My view is yes, you should, but with help in explaining who you are and why you do certain things. If you don't convey the real you and you fake it, the recipe is going to be a lifetime of depression and exhaustion.

Once you know who you are, appreciate who you are, and are able to be proud of who you are, you'll feel comfortable enough to be the real you in all situations. You may explain to people, "I'm the sort of person who ..." and explain your characteristics in terms of eye contact, the things that you can do, or your exhaustion in that situation.

But remember to think, "You have to accept me as who I am. You may not like some of those characteristics, but that's who I am."

In psychotherapy, I work on the concept of self with people with Asperger's beginning right at the teenage years. Be proud of you! We've developed a teenage program called "Moving to Manhood," and part of that is focused upon self-identity and self-worth not only in your abilities, but in terms of your personality. By being fake, you're also giving signals to people that are going to affect relationships. When they see behind the mask, they're going to leave you because you're not the person they thought they knew. If you are going to build relationships, it's important that you're true to yourself so you can find someone who loves you for who you are. It's not easy to just take that mask off; I think there needs to be someone to give support. The mask needs to go because it temporarily gives you success, but at terrible personal cost.

CRAIG: I'm starting to wonder if he already knows the answers to the questions that he's been asking. If he's wearing the masks, he must already be quite proficient at being able to do it.

DR. TONY: Yes. He knows what to do, but the problems are the exhaustion and the false persona. He's almost got a dual personality. That would be awful to live and cope with. There's a very good video by Maja Toudal from Denmark; she describes how she was so good at upholding the facade that people couldn't believe it when she was diagnosed. She said, "I will not allow people to see behind the mask." But it's exhausting. It's a successful coping strategy, but one I'd be very cautious about. In her book, *Pretending to Be Normal*, Liane Holliday Willey describes very clearly that coming "out of the closet" and being true

to who she really is has made a huge difference for her life in terms of happiness.

CRAIG: In the book, does she talk about how to do that? Is there a plan for how to do that?

DR. TONY: Liane is very vivacious and she just came out the closet and said, "This is me. You've got to accept me for who I am." Some have the confidence to do it, some people don't. It depends on their personality. I do recommend that this person get a mentor who can help: either a professional or somebody with Asperger's who's done the same thing.

Chapter Eleven

Getting and Keeping a Job

Chapter Eleven — Getting and Keeping a Job

"I've not done anything wrong. Can I do anything to prevent them from firing me?"

CRAIG: The next question says, "Hi, Dr. Tony. I am possibly the most successful salesman for my employer, having been nominated for the top sales award six times in eight years. Now, under a new manager, I face 'performance management'—a euphemism for firing me. They are using obscure behavioral standards to construct a case. Now, I have created a presentation to explain my behaviors to the team, but I've been given just ten minutes to present them. I have not done anything wrong and I have received praise from my customers. Can I do anything to prevent them from firing me?"

DR. TONY: This is a very important question. The official definition of Asperger's syndrome is "a person who has difficulty relating to their peers." That's crucial: peers. You are very good with your customers, I've know those with Asperger's who have been exceptionally good doctors and nurses and are wonderful with their patients. But it's with their peers they really find this a problem.

You've said the key words here in your question, "the team." Despite the fact that you are an exceptional salesperson—you know the script, you know what to do, you are very convincing—what they're saying is, "We don't understand you and we're not going to spend the time to understand you. It's easier to get rid of you." There are aspects of the interpersonal and team components in the workforce that may be confusing or annoying your workmates. Perhaps the manager is getting complaints from others, or doesn't understand you and would rather reject you than spend time to understand you.

Now, that would be a terrible waste of your talents! First of all, please don't see this as a fault in you. I think that your boss needs an understanding of what Asperger's is. Assuming you have a confirmed diagnosis, I'd suggest you prepare a document of just about two pages (to ensure it's read) on the characteristics of Asperger's:

why it makes you good in the job and how to support your peers in recognizing the challenges. There are a variety of books on employment. I suggest you read them, identify the key issues that are relevant to you, and then create a brief description of yourself.

CRAIG: Good luck. I hope you report back to us on how this goes. If you have talent and ability, my hunch is that they are going to try to find reasons to keep you. The more you can educate them as to how they can help support you, the more both of you will find success. That's great, Dr. T. Thank you.

"Finding a job for someone with developmental delays."

CRAIG: "My seventeen-year-old son is currently looking for work. He also has developmental delays. How will he go about getting a job or even choosing a career?"

DR. TONY: This is a tricky one. It's something we've recognized here in Australia for some time. The government is concerned that people should not be on welfare if they have the potential for employment, and the way I see it is that a good job is a better antidote to depression than medication! In Australia, and I would recommend this in other countries, the government has provided funding for employment agencies to specialize in autism spectrum disorders. Here, in Brisbane, we have three organizations. They have their staff trained in the area of autism and its whole range of expressions. They're able to find a job that's autism-friendly from sensory sensitivity to attitudes. They then support the person in their application, in rehearsing for the job interview, and when they are in the job. As far as the government's concerned, this is great because the person is now a taxpayer.

They really do need somebody who can speak to the advantages of employing the person with Asperger's. With my colleagues, Michelle Garnett and Jay, I am writing a program called Thriving Now (www.thrivingnow.net) to help those with Asperger's syndrome thrive in a job setting. It includes stress management, sensory issues, organization and planning, the social element, and more. It's composed of five three-hour sessions along with a workbook that goes through all the challenges Aspies in the workplace may face.

At the end of the program, you have a final workbook that you can use to explain the qualities you can offer and the challenges you may have to your employer. We're currently evaluating it; it should be available online. It's called "Thriving" because we recognize that too many of the adults we see are in despair due to unemployment. The thing is, many companies are interestingly very keen on changing their philosophies. In big banks and information technology, for example, they're realizing that such individuals can be very good employees and very helpful. There's a paradigm shift now for the employers of big companies. The CEOs are saying, "We have a corporate responsibility. We should train our staff in accommodating that."

For this particular family, it's going to be difficult, but I think they should go and have a look at some of the books that exist already. Temple Grandin has written an excellent one. I think they need to read what's being written, and then they will have to do the legwork and find the right job and support system.

"My son likes to work. What job programs might fit him?"

CRAIG: The next question has to do with finding a job and socializing. "Hi, Dr. Tony, I'm the mother of an eighteen-year-old, high-functioning ASD son. I'm trying to find out what job programs might best fit him. He did a six-week work program with a company; he loves waking up and going to work and earning a paycheck, but now that is over. My son also has issues with social skills.

"He can follow directions, but if he's doing something wrong and he's called out on it, he thinks that person is criticizing him. Is there a group that could help him socialize and maybe find a friend?" This person didn't say where they're from, but I'm assuming this is a universal phenomenon. Do you know of job programs and social groups in different parts of the world?

DR. TONY: What a good, good question, and how fortunate that I'm now working on that, again, with Michelle Garnett and Jay Hobbs. [laughs] The three of us are putting together a program called "Thriving Now." It's a five-session, downloadable program which involves video recordings of Michelle and I, a workbook to go through, and all sorts of background information.

If you go to mindsandhearts.net, there's a tab at the top there called "Thriving Now," and it's a five-session self-help book. I would recommend downloading that program to help him. It covers aspects such as social skills and sensitivity to making mistakes. That's one of the major things that we focus on during the program. The other resources I would recommend are a number of books published by Jessica Kingsley Publishers on helping people with ASD find and keep a job. The first problem is to get one, the next problem is to keep it.

Chapter Twelve

Disclosing a Diagnosis

Chapter Twelve — Disclosing a Diagnosis

"To tell or not to tell is quite an issue. Who needs to know?"

CRAIG: "Once somebody is diagnosed, how do they tell others about their autism?"

DR. TONY: To tell or not to tell is quite an issue. I think it needs to be reserved for those who need to know. For those who don't, I prefer to use phrases like, "I'm the sort of person who tends to look away when you're talking. I'm not being rude, it helps me concentrate on what you're saying," or "I'm the sort of person who talks and talks about trains. I'm so enthusiastic, but I'm not good at reading the signals of boredom. If I'm boring you, please interrupt me." Take the characteristics of Asperger's explain it as a description of your personality, rather than a syndrome.

If you tell others, you don't know if they'll keep that information confidential (if it needs to be confidential). Once it's out, you have no idea where it's going to go and who's going to take advantage of it. I think it's really a question of trust.

There may be certain people who could need to know for a purpose. For example, if the person with Asperger's is at risk of losing their job because of the characteristics of Asperger's, then they need to tell their employer. If there are issues for an adult in a relationship that could be causing friction or possible separation, then it's important that the partner knows. If it's to neighbors or colleagues at work, I would be cautious. I'd recommend you only tell those who need to know until you trust them.

Ask Dr. Tony

> **"Is there a bias against diagnosing people with Asperger's who are doing well?"**

CRAIG: "Dr. Tony, is there a bias against diagnosing people with Asperger's who are doing well? Doesn't this rob us of role models and mentors?"

DR. TONY: It's very true, actually. Clinicians usually only get those who have major difficulties coming through the door, otherwise they wouldn't be there. There are people I've known through the years who have had their issues in childhood or adolescence, and then I lose touch with them. Sometimes they only see someone when they're having problems, which gives a biased view. Yet there are some who are doing really well, and to a certain extent, they are what we call "subclinical": they've reached a point where the current diagnosing criteria don't necessarily explain their characteristics. Such individuals still have the core characteristics of AS, but they're not having a significant detrimental effect in their daily life. They are doing well, and they are heroes. I do encourage people who have those characteristics to explain to fellow Aspies the path they followed to become successful with the same characteristics.

> **"How can I learn to see my diagnosis as a gift or an opportunity rather than a downright curse?"**

CRAIG: This next woman describes how she was diagnosed as being on the spectrum when she was thirteen. Her parents told her teacher, but unfortunately, the teacher was one not quite as sensitive as he should have been. The young girl's psychologist recommended not telling her about her diagnosis quite yet.

Chapter Twelve — Disclosing a Diagnosis

The girl's teacher advised her of her diagnosis and used harsh words. He told her that she was damaged in the brain and that dreams of going to college were just setting her up for failure because people on the spectrum didn't have the mental capability for it. It's hard for me to imagine somebody was this harsh in a teaching situation, let alone this ignorant. He did make the statement that "if she worked hard, she may be able to achieve some small positive contributions to society."

Here's where the story gets encouraging. The girl states that her life has not turned out the way the teacher described, and she has achieved some degree of success. She still feels like a failure, and it's this failure that she's writing about.

"Dr. Tony, how can I get past this experience once and for all, so I don't feel ashamed of myself or feel like a constant failure? How can I learn to see my diagnosis as a gift or an opportunity rather than a downright curse?"

DR. TONY: In a way, I would support the psychologist's suggestion of not informing her of her diagnosis. Thirteen-year-olds are very sensitive to the concept of self and what they hear, especially from their peer group. Psychologically, they can be very fragile, and to give them that information without the proper support mechanisms can be a risky process. I would endorse what that psychologist originally said; the usual time to explain the diagnosis is after the teenage years. If you're going to give it at thirteen-, fourteen-, or fifteen-year-old when they're still evolving and going through the stages of transition, it's a very delicate stage psychologically.

The chances are, from the description, that teacher did not know about Asperger's and went to the web where he read inappropriate information and thought that this was the case. He thought he was giving her the facts when he told her she was someone who will never be successful. How someone could pass that information along thinking they're going to help, I have no idea; I'm a bit unsure of his motive at the time. However, that's inaccurate information.

When something is introduced to a teenager with Asperger's for the first time, that can be comparable to writing on a whiteboard with a permanent pen. Whoever writes on it first writes on it permanently, and the ASD individual sees no reason to change it—especially when it comes from someone with authority such as a teacher. From my perspective, I think that was terrible, devastating, and exactly what I would not want to happen.

Now, her life has not turned out that way; in fact, she has proven that person wrong. I think what you said at the end of your question is wonderful closure on this. I think you need to start seeing Asperger's syndrome as a gift. You're different.

I'm afraid you may have to wait until your peers grow up to really appreciate your qualities. For many with Asperger's, they may not blossom until the adult years. That's what I encourage you to do … see yourself as different. You did it! You proved that teacher wrong—and good on you for doing it! Well done!

CRAIG: Excellent. I love stories like that, too.

Chapter Twelve — Disclosing a Diagnosis

"Are there some good book about Asperger's for a nine-year-old?"

CRAIG: "Our nine-year-old son was recently diagnosed with high-functioning autism. He reads at an advanced level for his age, and we're trying to find a book that he can refer to that helps him understand in a non-patronizing way. I'm sure you have some book suggestions."

DR. TONY: The first book I would (obviously) recommend is my book, *Asperger's Syndrome: A Guide for Parents and Professionals.* I wrote it in a way that a person with a reading age of twelve or more should be able to understand it, which should work for your nine-year-old who enjoys reading. It is not too heavy, it is very accurate, and portrays a positive view.

DR. TONY: A friend of mine, Kathy Hoopmann, has written some excellent fiction for kids around the age of this particular child. She originally wrote the fiction story *Blue Bottle Mystery*; it would be very easy for him to read, probably in an hour or two, but the

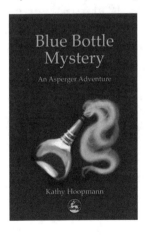

central character has Asperger's in a positive way and it's part of a trilogy. The next one is a great *Star Trek* spoof, but I would recommend this as bedtime reading.

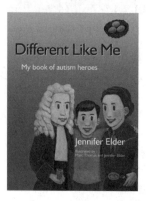

The interesting is that *Blue Bottle Mystery* is now in the format of cartoons. It's a science fiction of a fascinating world called Elemental Island, where all the Aspies have gone to for various reasons. Neurotypicals have been obliterated in a nuclear war, but Elemental Island remains and thrives. It's a story of what would life be like if Aspies were the vast majority of people.

There's a neurotypical born on the island, and it chronicles all the challenges of that type of environment. I would recommend *Elemental Island* as a great read. Another one is *Different Like Me*, it's a series of descriptions of famous people in history who had Asperger's characteristics, including Immanuel Kant, Sophie Germain, Pierre Von Trapp, Andy Kaufman, and Dian Fossey. He may recognize that in the sciences, the arts, and the caring professions, there have always been people with Asperger's syndrome.

Chapter Twelve — Disclosing a Diagnosis

"Once I do get diagnosed, I will have a hard time talking to my mom about it."

CRAIG: The next question is from somebody worried about other people learning of his diagnosis. "I'm thirty-eight years old and I have not been officially diagnosed yet, but I am in the process. Once I do get diagnosed, I will have a hard time talking to my mom about it. She thinks she knows it all and will be offended if I get a diagnosis. She will be in denial or take it personally. I'm a little upset that she didn't recognize my symptoms at a younger age, or get me actual help instead of sending me to institutions that didn't help." Clearly, this person has the feeling they're already on the spectrum and wishes mom would have seen this before.

DR. TONY: I think this is an increasing phenomenon, adults find out about Asperger's from the media and it seems to fit. Often, they've been to psychiatric services where something has been diagnosed—anxiety, for example. Then when reading about Asperger's, there's a light bulb moment of suddenly realizing, "Wow, that describes me perfectly." It's a revelation for the person. Now they've got to find a professional who also recognizes that and can complete the diagnostic assessment.

This person is thirty-eight years old; when he was at school, we did not know about Asperger's. That's not his mom's fault, she wouldn't have known. She would also have been guided by professional advice at the time. It's a paradigm shift for her in terms of Asperger's syndrome, because in her mind autism is a severely disabled, non-verbal, flapping, institutionalized person, and her son doesn't represent that. She needs to take time to process the information and to learn it. Hopefully, the person who conducts the diagnostic assessment would be able to talk to his mother, not only to give some degree of credibility to what her son is describing, but also change how she perceives and understands him. It's not going to be easy, but I think it is possible if her son can be patient with her.

Ask Dr. Tony

> **"The assessment process was absolutely devastating for both my daughter and me!"**

CRAIG: "For several years, I suspected that my twelve-year-old daughter might be an Asperger's girl. I accepted her for her differences because there were more strengths than weaknesses. However, things started to get tough at school and the school asked us to have her assessed. The assessment process was absolutely devastating for both my daughter and me.

"The tests and interviews seemed random and the questions scared her, causing her to come to me with questions such as, 'What's wrong with me?' or 'Why would they think I'd want to hurt animals?' She became so fearful of having autism that when the diagnosis came back and it was ASD mild to moderate, I couldn't tell her. I just said that the tests have helped us understand the way that she thinks a little better. She's extremely resistant to any type of workshops or therapy and she refuses to go anywhere near a psychologist after the testing process was completed. My question to you is, am I doing the wrong thing in not telling her about her diagnosis?"

DR. TONY: Oh, dear. What a shame, there was such a bad reaction to the person doing the diagnostic assessment that she's now scared of going to such people. I quite understand that her mother is unsure whether to confirm the diagnosis. I trust the mother's judgment, and if she feels that information would be catastrophic for her daughter, I would leave it be for the moment.

Also, there's another issue. Her daughter is twelve years old, and I find that explaining the diagnosis to those in adolescence may lead to them resisting it because they don't want to appear different. It's not that they disagree with the diagnosis necessarily, they just are desperate to fit in. They know what can happen if they have a disorder: there could be rejection, humiliation, bullying, and teasing.

Now, I think certain people need to know. The school needs to know. It's then kept as confidential information until Mom recognizes that there's the right time to explain it, and that may well be further down the track by several years. At this stage, leave it be.

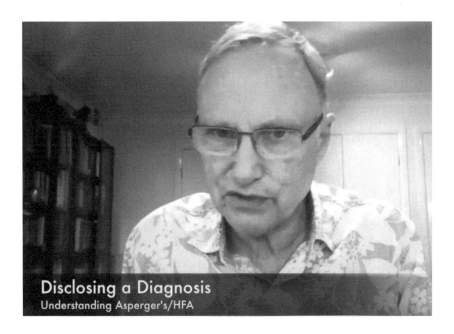

Disclosing a Diagnosis
Understanding Asperger's/HFA

Chapter Thirteen

Bullying

Chapter Thirteen — Bullying

"My Aspie relative bullies me. How do Asperger's and personality intermix?"

CRAIG: The next question says, "Dr. Tony, I have a close Aspie relative who has intentionally bullied me over the last year. In the past, he just acts like nothing has happened when he ultimately cools down, but he has withheld information, made false accusations about me, and sent me aggressive e-mail. I have three questions about him. How do Asperger's and personality intermix? Surely there are Aspies that are nicer than others. Is Asperger's a valid excuse for hurting others without consequence? What else can I do, apart from ignoring his rants?"

DR. TONY: Much of this depends on how the person reacts to being different and what their underlying personality is like. Some people, for example, hate the concept of Asperger's. They deny it. Others will say, "Well, that's me. I'm going to be positive about it." You get the optimists, you get the pessimists. You get those who are, by nature, calm and accommodating and avoidant of anger. Such behavior would never be in their thoughts at all. However, when you know one person with Asperger's, you know one person with Asperger's.

The personality does intermix, but what also intermixes are experiences: peer group comments that make each person with Asperger's unique. When I do an assessment, one of the questions I'm asking is, who's underneath the Asperger's? Some personalities are endearing, and it brings out that caring, kind instinct in other people. Unfortunately, there are those who, for various reasons, are abrasive and annoying to others due to what seems to be a personality component.

Is Asperger's a valid excuse for hurting others without any consequences? It is certainly not! Those with Asperger's usually want social justice and equality. It is very important that though Asperger's may cause difficulties, it does not make you immune from consequences. That's not only within a family, that's in law, and is also important at school. Whatever the school consequences are, that must occur—but it must be equal justice when all the information is disclosed. Otherwise, the amount of damage is indicative of the amount of guilt, and that may not be the case at all.

In this situation, I would want to know what is causing the antagonism. Sometimes, it can be a perceived injustice that's occurred, causing the Aspie individual to only see the things their relative is doing wrong. They're not using balanced perception, they only spot the mistakes. You must get them to re-perceive you. What I would do is go to that person and say, "Look, you are trying to control your life and avoid unpleasant situations to make your life easier, but the way you're doing it is bullying. It's a very powerful way of manipulating people. You can get what you want by being nice. If you are complimentary, you are supportive, and you are kind, you'll probably get more. If you want to control your environment, you can, but you don't have to do it by being mean and nasty." That's where the person must learn the nice way first, must be the recipient of that kindness. Following that, when he's nice, give him double of what he wants as encouragement.

Bullying

Chapter Thirteen — Bullying

CRAIG: It sounds like there is something that this person can do to help affect their relative's behavior. That's great.

DR. TONY: As I've mentioned before, my concern isn't Asperger's, it's neurotypicals and how they treat people with Asperger's. Unfortunately, bullying is a common experience for those with Asperger's syndrome. It can be a great cause of school refusal because school is a war zone; they think, "I'm going to be ambushed, I'm going to feel pain, discomfort, embarrassment, and humiliation. Why should I go to school?" The tragedy is they can start to believe it. They may not have had friends to correct or counterbalance that negativity, and then start to perceive the world and their experiences in the light of what the bullies would say. There may be a lack of friends who would serve as an antidote and as protection for that person. Those with Asperger's often need a logical explanation, but the bullying can still be relentless. Often, what we must do is explain the psychology of predators so that the person can have closure.

Continuing with strategies for bullying, it needs a team approach if you are dealing with somebody in a high-school setting. The silent majority, who are often around when bullying occurs, must be encouraged as much as possible to step in and stop it. It's not cool, it's not funny, everyone deserves to feel safe, and it can't be accepted.

What's needed is a response that is true and that will not inflame the situation. We were working with one group of teenagers with Asperger's, and one member's father is a police officer; he's very proud of his father. Another boy said, "Your father is a corrupt police officer," and we were about to work out how to respond when the first fellow said, "And your mother's a prostitute." I thought, "That's playing the game that you're bound to lose." I know it's tempting and impulsive to just say the first thought and get retaliation but, I'm sorry, you are going to lose that game.

Confide in someone you trust and explain what's occurring so they can repair the situation and support you. It's very important to remain calm and in control. Your talent is your intelligence, your challenge is your emotions. Don't let emotions take over.

Have safe havens you can go to, like a library. You need to achieve closure by knowing the motives of bullies, because if you can't have closure, the risk is replaying the event many years afterwards. It's still fresh in your memory and there can't be closure until you know why that happened.

"Dealing with bullies."

CRAIG: "There are some people, even members of my family, who are just plain bullies when it comes to the way they treat my ASD sister. They say nasty things and sometimes use her as a convenient target because they know she doesn't say anything back. It's overwhelming for her, she becomes intimidated and does not repel these attacks very well as she tends to freeze up. Then she feels bad because she feels she didn't handle a situation well. I've tried to explain to family members (with my sister's permission) why she is the way she is, and I've told them about her Asperger's with hope that it would make them more sympathetic to her. Sadly, it has not changed things. My question is, what is a good way for people on the spectrum to learn how to deal with bullies like these, especially when they're alone?"

DR. TONY: First of all, congratulate her for not retaliating. I think that's very wise. The trouble here is that she's believing them; she's taking in the suggestions that they make about her and she's thinking they must be real. However, what these relatives are really showing is that they have a poor ability to judge character. They can't see the qualities that she's got, the heroic way that she's coping, and there's none so blind as those who won't see. I'm sorry, you can't change them.

What you can do is try and repair some of the things that other family members have said, and tell her, "Look, they really don't understand you. Their comments aren't worth it. It's important not to get upset by it because people you value, people who have qualities like me, are those who really appreciate you and what we say counts more."

"Why do people bully?"

CRAIG: "My sixteen-year-old who has ASD is being bullied for being different. What should I do?"

DR. TONY: People bully someone who's different, and someone with autism and Asperger's is different by definition. If someone doesn't understand and value that person, then they may opt to have fun by bullying and teasing them. I find that, psychologically, what's far worse is rejection and humiliation. At sixteen, he's building his self-esteem and concept of self, and that can be devastating.

The people who bully, tease, reject, and humiliate have no idea of the damage they do. Sometimes, when a person with Asperger's meets their bully after a few years and has been thinking of what they did every day since, the bully may not remember doing or saying anything at all. Yet, the person with Asperger's remembers it so vividly and can't have closure because they can't understand why someone would intentionally hurt them.

Those with ASD are predominantly the victims of bullying and teasing because they're different and they're not going to be supported by popular friends. Often, those who bully them will get away with it and when the person with Asperger's retaliates they get into trouble. Bullying is something that can lead to depression and low self-esteem, and if it's at school the parent needs to talk to the school and say, "This is going to cause serious psychological harm to my child, and it needs to be stopped."

If we're going to stop it, we must encourage other kids to step in and help. Most of these actions happen when teachers aren't looking because students don't want to get caught; but the other kids are watching. Ask them to step in and put a stop to it. That's the only way it's going to occur: by the other kids saying, "It's not cool. It's not funny. It's cruel what you're doing, and we don't agree with it."

A sanction from a peer is going to be more powerful than a sanction from a teacher, who is viewed as the enemy at sixteen, anyway. It's got to be the peers—usually the athletes because they're praised. They're the ones who are likely to stop it.

Chapter Thirteen — Bullying

"How can my kid not be taken advantage of by bad people?"

CRAIG: "Doctor Tony, in the social group that I run I hear a lot of parent's concerns that their young adults may be taken advantage of for money and possessions. How can a person on the spectrum guard against people who may want to take advantage of them? Are there strategies that parents can employ to help decrease their young adult's vulnerability?"

DR. TONY: Neurotypicals have built-in radar to spot bad characters. Those with Asperger's tend to assume that other people are honest and have the same degree of integrity as they have. Neurotypicals say that's naïve, but I think that's actually a good quality. It's very difficult to teach a person with Asperger's when a person is disreputable. All I can suggest is that you help the person find someone who is very good at character assessment, and they can serve as the one who gives the green light or the red light as to whether to pursue something further. Anyone new will need to meet that guardian.

If it's a business meeting about signing away your mortgage for your house, then they need someone who is experienced in this area. If it's someone who is questionable in terms of taking advantage of that person sexually, they'll need someone else to accompany them for coffee so they assess whether the person is safe.

"How do I get accurately diagnosed for autism?"

CRAIG: For this edition of the Ask Dr. Tony program, we've had over forty questions submitted. Many of them fall into similar categories. The most common question is, "How do I get accurately diagnosed for autism?"

Ask Dr. Tony

The questions come from two groups of people: parents looking out for their children, and adults looking to get diagnosed themselves. The questions include: can I find a diagnosis tool online? Is there a good reference that I can read up on? What's involved with the diagnostic test? If I have to go to a professional to be tested, where do I look? These questions come from all over the world.

DR. TONY: I don't have an online reference that seems to be the definitive way of diagnosing. In a way, you need to interact with a child or adult in a diagnostic assessment. I don't have a particular online group other than possibly Simon Baron-Cohen's team at Cambridge University, the Autism Research Center.

They actually have a number of screening questionnaires online that are free to use. These aren't definitive diagnostic instruments, but they are fairly predictive of whether a diagnosis will be confirmed. Simon has been working on the AQ, or "autism quotient." He originally developed it for adults, then teenagers, then children. I would recommend the ARC, Autism Research Center University of Cambridge.

Chapter Fourteen

Choosing a Career

Chapter Fourteen — Choosing a Career

"I think those with autism and Asperger's know who likes them and understands them."

CRAIG: The next question is from a teacher. He says, "Hi, Dr. Tony. I am a teacher and I've recently discovered that I have AS. I am licensed for middle and high school programs, but I'm wondering if I should adjust to teaching at the middle levels, or as a college professor who can run on about a favorite subject and be finally accepted for eccentricity. What have you seen in your profession? What would you advise?"

DR. TONY: People with Asperger's syndrome can not only be very kind, but also very determined to help others. For them, the teaching profession is an ideal one, and one that I recommend for people with Asperger's. However, teenagers are toxic to those with Asperger's. They're toxic when you go to school with them as a peer, but they also seem to have a dislike of adults and their main aims in life are to give the teacher a nervous breakdown and to bankrupt their parents. [laughs]

I think this person has very sound judgment of knowing that younger children are more respectful and are likely to be more compliant. As a college professor, those in the class want to be there. Teenagers don't want to be there; you're like a jailer in a prison, and they hate you for it. If you're prepared to continue, I think you'd be a great teacher!

CRAIG: That's great advice. I hope they do either stay with the younger levels, or go into teaching college.

Ask Dr. Tony

"Can an Aspie make a good manager?"

CRAIG: The next question is about jobs. "Can an Aspie make a good manager? Do you know of successful stories? I was only diagnosed a year after a difficult job and four years of contracts, many of which were not renewed. Are there any good apps available for social skills? I don't catch some sarcasm and I'm still misinterpreting some body language. I also have minor eye contact irregularities. I cannot understand stress and I want to know how to work issues out when people are bored. I also have had some difficulty with a crying employee. I do have gallons of determination because I love my field and I can talk endlessly about it, but I must be a supervisor to get paid decently. Can an Aspie make a good manager?"

DR. TONY: The answer is yes! The issues are motivation and learning. Clearly, this person is highly motivated by learning. There are a couple of good books that I would recommend; the first is by Malcolm Johnson and it's entitled *Managing with Asperger Syndrome*. He became a manager with the knowledge of his own Asperger's characteristics and goes through strategies that may help.

Another one is by Ashley Stanford and it's called *Business for Aspies*. Both of these are published by Jessica Kingsley Publishers.

It's important to let people know that interpersonal relationships are not your strength, and to tell them how you manage these situations. This person mentioned somebody who was crying, for example; in that situation, all they may need is compassionate listening, not necessarily someone to fix

166

the problem. It would be beneficial to have an advisor who's a colleague, a partner, or family member who you can talk to about that problem. They may be able to give you advice. You can be a successful manager, but you're going to need information, knowledge, and advice.

"Aspies and lack of empathy: fact or fiction?"

CRAIG: "I was recently diagnosed, and I'm studying to become a psychologist in northern Europe. In an earlier episode, you mentioned that you knew several therapists with ASD. I have heard from my teachers that the best predictor for success is the person's empathy. I find this depressing since Aspies have problems with empathy. What do you think about this? I also wonder if you have some general advice for an Aspie regarding the challenges of becoming a therapist or psychologist."

DR. TONY: Well, first of all, congratulations on putting in the effort to study psychology. I think you may become an excellent psychologist. I'm hoping to get psychotherapy designed by Aspies for Aspies, because they really do understand. The problem is that neurotypicals don't understand Aspies.

I'm going to go through several points on this. This is one of my soapboxes. To say that those with Asperger's don't have empathy is a gross insult. There is a difficulty reading the subtle cues in facial expression, in particular when it comes to affection or compassion, which leads neurotypicals to accuse the person of lacking empathy. People with Asperger's can be some of the kindest people and extraordinarily sensitive once they read the signals. It's not a lack of empathy, it's a difficulty reading the signals.

Research has shown there are three types of empathy. There's cognitive empathy, which is "knowing." A person with Asperger's may have difficulty with this. There's emotional empathy, which is "feeling." Often, they can feel and sometimes they're oversensitive to that. If they choose social withdrawal, it's because they are overly sensitive to negative atmosphere and it's painful. "Compassionate empathy" is knowing how to respond. People with Asperger's have been observers of humans since they were little children, and so they became a psychologist at the age of three.

I've written the foreword in an excellent book called *Raising Martians: From Crash-landing to Leaving Home* by Dr. Joshua Muggleton. Joshua has Asperger's syndrome and he's training to be a psychologist. He has a remarkable insight into Asperger's syndrome.

I would encourage you to become a psychologist and I would also suggest that you abandon all the previous psychological theories, as they were designed for neurotypicals. Start developing your own psychology for Aspies. A very well-valued colleague of mine, Rachel, has Asperger's syndrome and she's a psychotherapist. I don't think the problem is you, it's your teachers only knowing the textbook understanding of Asperger's, not the real clinical experience.

CRAIG: Wow, so he can literally bring them into the current age just by talking to them as to who he is. That's wonderful.

DR. TONY: Yes. Often, the person with Asperger's may think of empathy by other channels. When we do tests by only reading the eyes, that channel is a difficult one. However, there are more channels than that to work out emotional atmosphere. I think some with Asperger's almost have a sixth sense of picking up things and may be oversensitive, but they can't tell you how they pick that up.

Chapter Fifteen

Empathetic Attunement

> **"How can I tell the difference between an emotional feeling and a sensory feeling?"**

CRAIG: "I read recently that when people experience emotions, they feel physical sensations in their body. Specific emotions cause a specific set of sensory feelings and this is how people identify which emotion they are feeling. I can describe, in theory, the physical sensations that represent an emotional state, but I cannot identify these sensations in myself. Therefore, I cannot identify my emotional state. My questions are, how do I identify which of my physical feelings are emotional feelings? Which are just sensory feelings? And, how can I differentiate these sensations?"

DR. TONY: Very important question. When I talk to adults with Asperger's, they often describe a mind-body distinction. Their mind, their intellect, and their thoughts seem to be detached from their body. This is a psychological component but also, we think, a neurological one.

There's a part of the brain called the amygdala, deep within the brain, which is responsible for scanning the sensory system for

danger and alerting the body for fight-or-flight. It also alerts the frontal lobe (the thinking part of the brain) of internal sensations, from when you need to go to the toilet to when you are becoming increasingly agitated and are about to have a meltdown. Because there's less white matter—that is, neural connections between the amygdala and frontal lobe as a warning system—Aspies often don't realize this until the explosion is already out of control.

So, the frontal lobe, the thinking part of the brain, is often not connected to or communicating with the internal parts of the body. When you ask someone with Asperger's, "How are you feeling now?" They'll often say, "I don't know." And they're not being obtuse. That insight isn't only the ability to work out what others are thinking and feeling, but what you're thinking and feeling yourself.

What we try and do is clue a person in on some of the bodily sensations. For example, when you get agitated, anxious, or angry, your heart rate increases. So, we'll use a device that monitors heart rate through the day, or in particular situations, and note when the heart rate has reached a high level. What is the body feeling then? Perspiration, an audible heartbeat, etc. That signifies stress or anxiety.

You may need someone to work through how to identify the internal signals cognitively, because that not only acts as a warning system in various ways but also allows you to be in touch with the feelings that can help you in many ways.

"I think those with autism and Asperger's know who likes them and understands them."

CRAIG: "In one of his interviews, Dr. Tony said, 'I think those with autism and Asperger's know who likes them and understands them.

Chapter Fifteen — Empathetic Attunement

They know intuitively within five or ten seconds of meeting them.' I do not fully understand it. How can some people on the spectrum have an attuned instinct in cases like that, yet have difficulties in situations where I would expect that same instinct should help?"

DR. TONY: I have the same problem. [laughs] You're absolutely right. This seems illogical, mutually exclusive. I think what those individuals are doing is using a different channel than the usual approach of reading facial expression or body language. This is a basic primeval intuition that animals use to watch out for predators. It's also born of experience with people they have identified as nice to them and those who aren't. What we find is, when it comes to cognitive assessment of reading people's thoughts, feelings, and intentions, these individuals have great difficulty. But there seems to be many channels to acquire this skill.

Sometimes, I talk to adults and they say, "I'll walk into a room and have a feeling that there's a negativity here, and I just walk out." They're pretty good at finding out who likes them and doesn't like them.

"Am I overreacting?"

CRAIG: "Dr. Tony, how can I tell if other people are treating me badly or if I'm just overreacting to their behavior?" He's describing a workplace situation where his boss appeared to be venting, but he's not sure.

DR. TONY: I think there are three factors here. One is a tendency to personalize events. In other words, somebody could be in a bad mood. A person with Asperger's might think, "What have I done to cause their bad mood?" without realizing that person's car wouldn't start, they couldn't pay their mortgage, etc. There's a tendency to think, "It's something to do with me." The second is that people with Asperger's can be very sensitive to emotional atmosphere and if somebody is in a bad mood, there's sometimes an overreaction to negativity in other people.

If he thinks that his boss (or anyone else) is treating him badly, he needs more information and to start working on some phrases like, "I'm confused, are you annoyed with me?" or "I'm sensitive to what you say, I pick up annoyance. Is it something I have done?" Yes, it is a genuine problem, but you need more information from the person. Work out what I call a "spoken *Social Story*™" (developed by Carol Gray) that gets you more information as to how that person is feeling, and subsequently, what to do. Just ask them.

Chapter Sixteen

Being Diagnosed

Chapter Sixteen — Being Diagnosed

"Why would a diagnosis be important for my twelve-year-old daughter?"

CRAIG: "Hi Dr. Tony, I'm the mother of a twelve-year-old girl who's been undergoing assessment for the last two years with no diagnosis. Her ADOS and Gillberg tests came back inconclusive. Whenever I mention the need for a diagnosis, I am treated like a neurotic mother. I've been told that a diagnosis won't make any difference and that my daughter will still be my daughter. However, she dropped out of school a month after starting comprehensive. I'm upset with the school for not recognizing or understanding her difficulty in coping. I feel my daughter will need a diagnosis to help her understand herself; she already knows she's different from her peers and she has started to ask why. Am I being a neurotic mother or is a diagnosis really important?"

DR. TONY: A diagnosis is extremely important. We tend to find that classic autism is diagnosed in the preschool years, and while Asperger's is typically diagnosed in boys at elementary school age,

girls tend to be at the high school age. Girls are better at camouflaging their social difficulties; in other words, girls are very good at hiding being different. The ADOS and the Gillberg criteria are really standardized on the boys' expression, not the girls' expression, so I wouldn't necessarily use those as the ultimate instruments for a diagnostic assessment.

Would it make a difference? Yes. She's twelve years old and she's starting to realize that she is different, and the psychological consequences can be depression, anger, etc. She needs a diagnostic assessment by someone who is experienced in girls and women. As this person is in the United Kingdom, Dr. Judith Gould has specialized in girls and women with Asperger's syndrome and she may be able to recommend someone who could help in that area. Go ahead and seek that diagnostic assessment.

"Why should someone be diagnosed? At what age?"

CRAIG: "Throughout my life, I've had a great deal of difficulty dealing with people in both my private life and professionally. I've really struggled to communicate, which has caused me to become depressed and to withdraw even more. I have a four-year-old son who I suspect of having Asperger's. I believe I may have it as well. As an adult, should I be assessed? How can I go about being assessed?"

Now, I'd like to combine this question with a few others. "Do you need to be diagnosed? Isn't there a possibly that it could be used against you if you're looking for a job? What are your thoughts about being diagnosed as an older person? Does age help an Aspie find their feet in the NT world?"

Chapter Sixteen — Being Diagnosed

DR. TONY: Let's look at the first one: "As an adult, how would I go about getting assessed for autism or Asperger's syndrome?" It's really a question of choosing who to go to. I know many people are reluctant to go to a psychiatrist because they're not mentally ill and they don't want to be prescribed medication. The real question is, "Who do I go to that understands and won't project characteristics onto me that I don't have?"

Some individuals with Asperger's who have tried to get a diagnostic assessment in the past have received diagnoses that are partially accurate, such as anxiety or depression, but not fully accurate. You need to see someone who is experienced in the adult profile and how someone with Asperger's may have camouflaged their social confusion. They need to have seen at least fifty or more adults—for women, at least fifty women with Asperger's syndrome—to be able to understand the characteristics, because most of the literature is based on children. Whether you're seeing a clinical psychologist or somebody from an autism association, they must have broad experience.

I diagnose older individuals regularly at my clinic. I often ask the person, "When would you have liked the diagnosis to be confirmed?" The vast majority say, "As young as possible. Then people would have understood me." What the diagnosis often does is explain traumas of the past: why you were bullied and teased, why you would say things that would upset people when that was not your intention. Suddenly, many of these questions are answered. That could be a resolution of past issues. No matter what your age (I've diagnosed people in their eighties), a diagnosis can bring closure.

You can also better understand yourself, your strengths, and your weaknesses to help you decide what to do in terms of career and relationships. It will help you to feel less depressed, because you're no longer artificially acting like someone you're not. It also helps you find your way in the Aspie world because you can meet people in the Asperger's community who could be your mentors.

When it comes to jobs, I think you should be very cautious. If there are a lot of people applying for a job, whoever is sorting through the applications is thinking of reasons to reject. If there are a handful of people applying for one job, and the hiring manager doesn't know anything about Asperger's, it could give them a reason to reject your resume. Be very careful about doing that. There's no job or profession that should be impossible for someone with Asperger's, I've known of Aspies in all sorts of areas, including psychology and psychiatry.

It's up to the person to decide whether disclosure of their diagnosis will be to their advantage or detriment. If it's to your detriment, then don't disclose it. You don't have to. If you do disclose it, it must be done in a positive way that highlights how your Asperger's characteristics will be a benefit in this job, and also how the business can support you to develop your abilities.

CRAIG: I've heard you say in past conversations that knowledge is power. So, why not learn if you're in this position? Because if you are in this position, rather than being a second-rate NT, why not be a first-rate Aspie?

DR. TONY: Oh, absolutely.

CRAIG: I just think that bears reinforcing.

Chapter Sixteen — Being Diagnosed

"My son doesn't perceive himself as being different ... but he is."

CRAIG: "My eight-year-old son was diagnosed with Asperger's two years ago and he seems not to perceive himself as being different from other children. He does not know his diagnosis at this point in time, but when he gets upset he sometimes cries things like, "I want to be dead, I will jump out of this window." One time I actually had to pick him up off the windowsill where he stood glaring in my direction. I really don't know what to do about this, is there something I can do?"

DR. TONY: There are two different issues here: one is that he doesn't see himself as different, so if you talk about a diagnosis it will go in one ear and out the other. You have a separate issue here, which is a tendency to catastrophize with emotions, and that's part of ASD. When he gets an emotion it tends to be in maximum volume. If he's anxious, he'll hit the panic button. If he's feeling sad, he hits the suicide button. When he says things like that, it is a genuine reflection of the intensity of his emotions.

What tends to occur is that they're okay until something happens that upsets them, and then they catastrophize. The interesting thing is that half an hour later, he could be just fine, as though nothing had happened. When he goes into that state, don't take it too much to heart. Yes, he is genuinely upset and you need to watch him—but don't necessarily ask what's the matter, because at this stage he's so upset that he's not going to give you a coherent answer.

You can say something like, "You're very upset. If you can live with it, it'll be over in half an hour. I'm with you, I will stay with you, I love you, and I will support you." Eventually, like a summer storm, will blow itself out. Meanwhile, Mom's been quite upset for a long time because if a typical kid gets to that degree of reaction, it means it's an extreme condition. This is the tendency within Asperger's, to have very intense emotions.

She needs to work with him to find out what the triggers for that intense emotion are—failure, imperfections, criticism, teasing, laughing—and then go through them with him.

"Is it worth taking my child off his meds to get a diagnosis?"

CRAIG: The next question is from a woman in Germany, her ten-year-old son is exhibiting some behaviors that require medication. If they try to remove these medications, things get pretty dicey. "I would like very much to have my child evaluated for autism, but that will require the removal of his medications. My question to you is, is it worth removing him from the medications and going through the trials in order to be able to have a known diagnosis of autism?"

DR. TONY: My simple answer is yes, but your son needs to be part of the decision making. For that time when he's off the medication, he is going to show how he feels about going through a difficult time. I think that at school he is well-behaved and responsive, almost not having the signs of needing that medication. To convince people that there is a genuine underlying problem, it may be necessary for a week or two to not take the medication. Your son needs to be very much involved in why this is occurring; it's because people need to know to help understand his genuine difficulties.

CRAIG: What sort of things would you tell her son to help convince him that this is worthwhile?

DR. TONY: Things like, "You are so good at school and people are amazed by your capabilities, but they may not understand how hard you work to get that degree of achievement. They need to see you without the help to see how far you've traveled, and your achievements in being able to manage not only your behavior but also concentration."

"My mother was just diagnosed at eighty-three. Can I help her understand?"

CRAIG: "After I was diagnosed at forty-three, my eighty-three-year-old mother read five chapters of *Aspergirls* and diagnosed herself as being on the spectrum. What can I do to help make her aware of important AS information that would help us both without bombarding and confusing her at this point in her life?" What a compassionate, considerate thing!

DR. TONY: This may explain a lot of things for this person and their mother, and better late than never! They can now make peace with themselves and other people. I think that's very important. They're discovering a lot about themselves, and they will have things in common and things that are different; it's just like jigsaw puzzle pieces, and they're finding out which pieces are similar and which aren't. Go through that voyage of discovery with her, that's what the pieces will explain: why you did certain things when you were a kid, and why people reacted in a particular way.

Your mother can do this as a personal exercise to make sense of the world. It also may mean that she could repair bridges with various people, especially family members who may not understand her. Now you can explain, "Mom's just not reading the signals, she's doing it this particular way." It may help your mother, and other family members may now appreciate who she is and what she's faced.

CRAIG: Well, it's just such a wonderful opportunity for this person to sit down with her mother and share that rapport. I'm impressed by how compassionate they are and that they're thinking of their mother in this regard.

DR. TONY: I'm going to add more to that. When I'm meeting somebody in their seventies or eighties for the first diagnosis I will say to them, "If you could turn back time, what would you do differently? There are things you did that succeeded, and there are things that didn't. We need that wisdom, you're a wise elder in the cultural tribe of Asperger's, and we need to pass that on. What would have helped when you were sixteen years old? What would have helped you then when you were twenty-five? When you got married? When you had kids? What worked and what didn't work? I need to take note of that, because I want to make sure those following you have the advantage of your experience."

CRAIG: I wish there was some way we could start an archive of thoughts like that, wisdom from the elderly.

DR. TONY: It needs to be captured and passed on. The idea of suicide comes to those who are depressed because their view is, "It will never get better, I'll always be like this." They need to talk to people who say, "It does get better. I thought, like you, I would never get a job or could never have a relationship. But it really could happen."

That is far more credible than anything I could say as a psychologist: when somebody who's been through what they're dealing with (or maybe worse) says, "I have a much better life now, I've come to terms with myself and am at peace with various things. I forgive those who are mean to me, I've moved on, I'm enjoying life." They need to see that, they need to hear it, they need to feel it, otherwise they feel that things are never going to get better.

Chapter Sixteen — Being Diagnosed

NOTE: The book *Been There. Done That. Try This!* including the combined wisdom of over twenty-five Aspie mentors was produced in response to this conversation in 2013.

> *"My friend insists, 'I don't have your disease,' despite how many people behind his back might say that he's a poster person for AS."*

CRAIG: "When I first read about AS years ago, I immediately thought of my friend. He didn't want to hear about it then. Many years later, I found out that myself, a family member, and some other acquaintances all are on the spectrum. However, my friend refuses to even look at the materials and insists, 'I don't have your disease,' despite how many people behind his back might say that he's a poster person for AS."

I want to help connect him with the local AS resources that have helped me but he would have to be motivated on his own, as I cannot change his mind for him. It is really frustrating to hear him go on about issues that I know that there's help for, if he would even think of screening himself. Do you have any advice?"

DR. TONY: I like the quote "I don't have your disease," and I think this give me an enormous amount of information. It may well be that this person considers ASD a mental disturbance, or somebody who is defective. In other words, he's got a very bad perception of what it is, and he doesn't want to have it. It's very possible this person has actually known that they were different from other people, probably from when they were very young. The quite understandable way of compensating for that is to see yourself as perfectly normal, which is more to convince yourself than other people.

It's comforting for him to think that, while other people may have their issues, they don't apply to him. He's not going to accept anybody challenging the structure that has given him comfort and support through the decades, so I ask you to be patient. However, do take the time for him in the future when he needs help. It may be in terms of underachieving in his career, or when he's seeking a relationship—the issue here is going to be self-understanding, rather than denying. At this stage, just be patient.

CRAIG: I also want to give this person credit for being compassionate and doing a favor for their friend here. That's remarkable. Good for them.

"What's going to happen when the term 'Asperger's' disappears?"

CRAIG: "Since the term Asperger's is going to disappear and it will no longer be an official diagnosis, does that mean that people who have already been diagnosed are going to be, for lack of a better way to say it, considered 'cured' and no longer qualify for the support they may be needing? How will it affect those that are diagnosed with Asperger's in 2013?"

DR. TONY: My understanding is that the descriptions of Asperger's syndrome will still be absorbed into the new system; the term will not be "Asperger's syndrome" but "autism spectrum disorder level one." All the characteristics that we use for the diagnosis will be there, but the wording will change. That's not a question of being cured. The assumption would be that those who have a diagnosis of Asperger's syndrome would then be diagnosed with ASD level one, as they only change the terminology.

Chapter Sixteen — Being Diagnosed

I have major issues with the term "level one" and I do think the term "Asperger's syndrome" should be continued clinically for a variety of reasons. However, the question at hand is whether those individuals will no longer qualify for support. They may, but my concern is if you use the term "level one," certain organizations may interpret the words "level one" as meaning "does not need government-funded support," which has already occurred in Australia. I am very concerned about replacing Asperger's syndrome with ASD level one.

CRAIG: Is there something we can do as a population who has invested in this name and finds it as a form of identification? Is there something we can do to help that panel to take a closer look at whether or not the name should go away?

DR. TONY: I think that's very important, because they need to realize the consequences of what they're doing outside of the isolation of a committee room. The American Psychiatric Association has a web page, and you can send them messages of your personal thoughts of the changes.

"What's the difference between autism and personality disorders?"

CRAIG: "I have autism. I don't really get the differences and connections between autism and personality disorders. Are they something completely different, or are there connections? And if these connections exist, what are they, and to which personality disorders do they connect?"

DR. TONY: There are two dimensions to this. One is history. People with Asperger's are not psychotic or intellectually disabled, but clinicians will have met them for various reasons and used their training to describe some characteristics with terms like "schizoid personality disorder" or "nonverbal learning disorder." And so, historically, such individuals have been placed into a personality category. The other dimension is how an individual copes with having Asperger's syndrome.

Some can become quite arrogant as a compensation mechanism for not fitting in. They soothe and support themselves by saying, "I'm better than other people." Then, they're accused of having narcissistic personality disorder. There can be other things, too: a fear of rejection, intense emotions, or despair, which lead to being viewed as having borderline personality disorder. It's how you've reacted to the situation.

I think that in many ways it's historical and how an individual has adapted. Sometimes the adaptations to Asperger's, if they're not positive and constructive, can lead to the development of a personality disorder.

Being Diagnosed with Asperger's/HFA
Avoidant Personality Disorder/Social Anxiety Disorder

Chapter Sixteen — Being Diagnosed

"How do Asperger's/HFA, avoidant personality disorder, and social anxiety disorder correlate?"

CRAIG: "My highly intelligent husband is about to be diagnosed with avoidant personality disorder but also has many traits that are applicable to social anxiety disorder. In reading all of the Asperger's blogs, I recognized that Asperger's aspects are a part of his character. How do Asperger's, avoidant personality, and social anxiety correlate? How can each of them be distinguished?"

DR. TONY: Very, very good question. We're talking here about avoidant personality disorder. One of my concerns is that once a person is recognized as having autism spectrum disorder or they know that they're different, subsequent to that, they can develop a personality disorder as a way to adjust. Sometimes it's narcissistic, sometimes it's multiple personalities ... the avoidant personality is important because it describes someone who feels inadequate in social situations. They will be very sensitive to negative evaluation and have a fear of criticism, disapproval, rejection, and being shamed or ridiculed.

My perspective is that this is a personality disorder, but also a reaction to a peer group throughout childhood. We talk about bullying and teasing and how it's horrible in many ways, but clinically, I have found what is far more hurtful and pathological is humiliation, rejection, and feeling foolish. The person may begin to anticipate being met with disapproval or criticism in many situations. That's external, but another thing that can occur is self-criticism.

There's fear of making a mistake, having low self-esteem, and setting themselves up with a filter system in their perception of things. Anything that is ambiguous is then perceived as derogatory and negative (thinking, "They're looking at me!" when actually they just happen to be looking past your shoulder). Now, that can explain its origins. The question is, what do we do? Here, the person clearly needs positive feedback for the social engagement they have. When you're socializing, you don't get a round of applause, you don't get a tick in the box. You just have to assume you're doing okay.

It means that if this is a description of a husband, the wife could sometimes give him a script of what's going to happen and what's going to be said. Every so often in the social engagement, give him feedback of what he's done right. This will help improve his abilities, but more importantly, improve confidence. He needs much more positive feedback and someone there to guide him.

"What's the difference between autism and psychosis?"

CRAIG: The next question has to do with psychosis. "Dr. Tony, I'm looking for information about autism and psychosis for my brother. He's been on antipsychotic medication for many years."

DR. TONY: The level of psychosis in autism spectrum disorder is the same as in the general population, one in fifty are likely to develop a psychosis. What is a psychosis? In a way, it's delusions and hallucinations. The Aspie way of thinking can be very rigid, one-track, and almost delusional. It also means that in a disturbance of reality, those with Asperger's are very good at logic but not very good with emotions. When emotions are powerful, logic disintegrates. The person may appear psychotic because their anxiety, depression, or anger is so great that it's a disturbance of reality.

That intense emotion prevents grounded, positive, logical thinking. Usually, antipsychotic medication is prescribed in ASD not to treat psychosis, but as a sedative: it's to knock the person out and take away the energy as a matter of expediency. To help that person cope or family members cope with them, the medication sedates, but it's not prescribed to treat clear symptoms of psychosis.

It's often prescribed for reasons different from its original design. My concern is that we have no idea of the long-term effects of such medication. Speaking from forty years of clinical experience, if you're coming off antipsychotic medication, you must come off very, very slowly.

It also means that the medication has acted as a suppressant for emotions; the brain's natural way of coping with emotions, psychologically and biochemically, has been artificially adjusted by the medication. You're going to get a rebound effect, so the medication must be reduced slowly. If he's been on an antipsychotic for many years, it will take several years for him to come off it. I am thinking it may be helpful to him, but it must be reduced slowly and alternative strategies for emotion management must be provided.

"I have Asperger's. Will my kids have it?"

CRAIG: This next question also has two parts. "I don't know what to do. I have Asperger's. When I get older and I am looking for a wife, how will I tell her I have it? Will my kid have it?"

DR. TONY: If you meet your future wife, she's likely to fall in love with many of the positive aspects of Asperger's syndrome and she will initially find those highly endearing. That's one of the reasons she'll fall in love with you. However, there may be other aspects that are missing or confusing and she will start to realize there are certain qualitative differences.

My advice is to try to explain your Asperger's fairly early on and to explain the positive components, i.e., "It makes me a very loyal person. I will be very dedicated to the relationship, but sometimes I may have difficulty knowing how to respond to your emotions, and sometimes I seem to be so focused on what I'm doing I've missed that I need to be doing things for you."

The next question is whether your kids may have Asperger's. There is no test at the moment, but in half the cases I see there is a family history of Asperger's-like features. What I would ask the couple to do is construct a family tree of both sides, and for each person in

that family tree come up with a score from zero to a hundred as to how Aspie they may be. You can then see what geneticists call penetration: how many people throughout the various generations have those characteristics to look at the statistical risks of recurrence.

With any child, we wouldn't know if they're on the spectrum until they're at least three to four years old. Whether you would have a subsequent child with those characteristics may be a possibility. There's a lovely quote from Dr. Stephen Shore when asked about he and his wife having children, and he said, "Oh no, we don't want children. They could be neurotypical."

CRAIG: [laughs] Somehow, I knew when you said Stephen Shore there was something like that coming. That's beautiful.

Chapter Sixteen — Being Diagnosed

"How do self-diagnosed Aspies get support and references when they get into trouble with officials?"

CRAIG: "Hi Professor Attwood, I'm undiagnosed. I had an experience with bad doctors and I fear being misdiagnosed. I'd like to be diagnosed someday by someone I trust, like you. How do self-diagnosed Aspies with no doctors or Aspie friends get support and references when they get into trouble with officials?"

DR. TONY: Sometimes the diagnostic professions can be incredibly conservative and may not recognize the characteristics of Asperger's, especially in someone at the upper ranges of ability. Their concept of autism spectrum disorders is someone who is quite significantly disabled, and you don't fit their schema of the type of person that they've met previously. I do recommend trying to find someone who's had experience with at least 100 adults with Asperger's syndrome to understand the variations in adaptation.

If this person is getting into trouble with officials, I don't know quite what the problem is there, but it does mean that there needs to be a degree of understanding and that the diagnosis needs to be confirmed. All I can hope is that they will find someone who knows ASD well. If not, they're going to have to travel; it may be worth traveling to a center of excellence to get that official paper.

"Doctor doesn't know if I'm Asperger's or a neurotypical with Aspie traits."

CRAIG: "The doctor who wouldn't diagnose me said he couldn't determine whether I'm a person with Asperger's who copes very well, or a neurotypical who's acquired some Asperger's-like traits. I will succeed in some social situations eight out of ten times, but every time I do nobody is more surprised than me. I have to work up to it every time and there's always the split second in which I wonder if it will work—and I can never be sure if it will work the next time. I used to get so mad at myself for not learning how to communicate with others. I thought after the sixth, seventh, or even seventeenth time I ought to know how it works, but I don't. It still feels like I've never done it before. Is this common in people on the spectrum? I tend to think that my brain is like a bathtub with no stopper, social skills-wise anyway, everything I put in runs out the other end, leaving some puddles—though the puddles make me hopeful."

DR. TONY: In a way, understanding social rules (what people are thinking exactly) is like learning a foreign language. When you learn a foreign language, you learn that there are always exceptions. People who learn English as a second language always complain of the exceptions. It is a language that's been combined by many different influences, and the exceptions will leave you quite bewildered. That's what happens with social interactions.

It can be frustrating if you think you've finally gotten it right, but it feels like the rules are always changing. The problem here is that it's not just being social, it's also has a lot to do with personality—and that's a whole new ballgame. The personality of each individual is different. That's why, with Asperger's syndrome, I'm very keen on teaching such individuals how personality affects what you do and how you act, and how to adjust what you're doing to the personality of the person. It's very much a work in progress.

All I can do is encourage you to keep going. The problem isn't you, it's the fickle, inconsistent, emotional, personality-driven neurotypicals.

Chapter Sixteen — Being Diagnosed

CRAIG: "My father is quite clearly an Aspie, though he's never been formally diagnosed. This has impacted my mother as well as my brother and me. I wonder how much of Asperger's responses are learned and copied by the children of an Asperger's parent? As children learn by example, is it possible they may exhibit some behaviors via osmosis and example rather than being Asperger's themselves?"

DR. TONY: You're spot on there. Asperger's syndrome is infectious. The more you live with or work with Aspie people, the more Aspie you become. To a certain extent within the family, it's a survival mechanism for neurotypicals. Quite often the Asperger's characteristics, especially in a father, can be the dominant force in the family. Sometimes you have to fall into line and adopt the same pattern of less social life, rigid routines, or other pieces of an Aspie lifestyle to survive. We find that when the children go and visit other families with their friends, they say, "Wow, this family is totally different. There's a very different atmosphere and routine. I feel quite comfortable here." That's something that I did in my childhood because I would visit other families and my mother would say, "Anthony, you'll wear your welcome out." "No," I said, because I wanted to be in a normal family.

In some ways, I think what you have is someone who can be different and remain true to their neurotypical self at school and at other people's homes, but when they go into the Aspie household they put the Aspie mask on to succeed in that environment. The children in that environment may also do the same to be able to create an atmosphere of home and cohesion that accommodates the Aspie characteristics.

Ask Dr. Tony

CRAIG: "Dear Dr. Attwood. My daughter is now seven years old and has had social problems since kindergarten. We have decided to seek a diagnosis for her. I was diagnosed with Asperger's last year and she shows a lot of signs of autism as well. The psychologist said she very clearly shows autism as well as ADHD, but she can't diagnose her because her autism might be learned from me. The thought that I might have taught her not to be able to read others' emotions and social signs dismays me. How probable is it that her behavior is learned? Am I at fault?"

DR. TONY: Another good question. As a clinician, what I'd be looking at is how your daughter interacts with her peer group, or with her peer group away from you. She may have learned to adapt to your particular style as you may have an Aspie household, in which case she learns the conventions and rules about Aspie households and how she needs to act in one, but that may not be her natural self. With a peer group on the playground or in the classroom, she may show the neurotypical pattern. At the age of seven, I doubt that it's imitation. It's more likely to be the genuine article. I really would ask that psychologist to observe your daughter in the school setting, which will be the real test of those characteristics.

CRAIG: "Is there a directory people can access to find where in the world they could go to have a formal test done?"

DR. TONY: I think that's a good idea. Regarding professionals, one of the key features is whether the person with autism develops a rapport with the diagnostician. If they don't they're going to shut down, and you don't know if that's due to autism or a dislike for the person who is assessing them.

Obviously, the more experience they have, the better they are at knowing what to look for. For children, I try and engage in play and interaction, and sometimes use particular instruments.

I would like there to be a directory because I get so many emails from people all over the world saying, "Who do you recommend in Madagascar? Who do you recommend in Ethiopia?" I'm sorry, I don't have anyone to recommend.

CRAIG: Okay, and the next question is, "What does a formal test look like? What's involved in it? Are there different varieties of tests? Can somebody be prepared for the some of the questions that are going to be asked?"

DR. TONY: The diagnostic criteria are in DSM-5, Diagnostic and Statistical Manual. You may be able to get that online and look at the criteria to get some idea of the areas that are going to be explored in a diagnostic assessment. I use an instrument which is still under development in which there are specific questions in relation to components of DSM-5.

Simon Baron-Cohen has developed the AQ, an excellent instrument, to really indicate a reasonable chance of diagnosis, but I tend to use

the Ritvo Autism Asperger Diagnostic Schedule Revised (RAADS). For adults, I would normally go through developmental history to start off: when did you know you were different? What differences were there? How did you do in elementary school, in friendships, schoolwork, etc.?

I walk through their developmental history, how they consider themselves different from other people, and the challenges they face in daily life. Now, throughout that process, I'm getting an assessment of nonverbal communication, understanding reciprocity, the interaction, and really getting a lot of information. I suppose in my mind, I have literally thousands upon thousands of people who have had a confirmed diagnosis.

I'm looking for patterns and consistency. If you have an experienced professional, they do this very quickly. Sometimes, for me, it's just a matter of minutes. For some, it is much longer, because they've got to disentangle whether it could be depression, PTSD, etc. Those are the tricky ones, along with girls and women. Even if I do know immediately, I've still got to do the formal process, and that will take two or three hours before I'm sure.

CRAIG: There's another question. This is specific. "Is there an age that is best to have the test begin, and is there an age at which nobody has to take it anymore?"

DR. TONY: I think the features are there for Asperger's syndrome in the preschool years, but we're not really that accurate in diagnosing it. If you know what to look for, you can see the very subtle differences but you really need someone who knows about typical development and the slight deviations—especially in girls. For adults, often the assessment is for personal needs rather than necessity to access services.

A diagnosis can provide closure with the past: why you were bullied and teased, why you thought you were crazy or stupid. It can also help you to make decisions for the future based on strengths.

Chapter Sixteen — Being Diagnosed

How have you coped with being different? Have some of those strategies helped you, and are some actually leading to low self-esteem/depression? For the adults, we go through their lifestyle and how the diagnosis could be an advantage to them.

> ## "How do I make an appointment to see you, Dr. Tony?"

CRAIG: This question is from somebody in New Zealand, which is quite close to you. "I live in New Zealand. How can I get an appointment to come and see you in person? I'm fifty-three, self-diagnosed three years or so ago, and I'm coming to terms with my current and past life." Do you take personal appointments from people?

DR. TONY: New Zealand isn't too far away. Sometimes, on Wednesdays, my friend and colleague Dr. Michelle Garnett and I do diagnostic assessments for difficult diagnoses at the Minds and Hearts

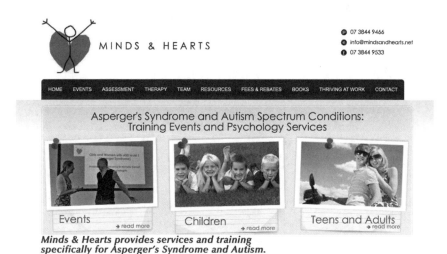

Minds & Hearts provides services and training specifically for Asperger's Syndrome and Autism.

Clinic in Brisbane. We spend the morning with one person and the afternoon with another. I would recommend they go to the webpage mindsandhearts.net and check the clinic on a Wednesday for Tony and Michelle.

CRAIG: Just out of curiosity, are you training other psychologists and psychiatrists to do testing yourself?

DR. TONY: All the time. There is nearly always someone sitting in whenever I do a clinic. It is very rare for me to do a clinic session on my own. I train clinical students, colleagues sit in, and sometimes people from abroad come along to see the process. There is nearly always someone sitting in and taking copious notes.

Chapter Seventeen

Living with Autism

Chapter Seventeen — Living with Autism

CRAIG: The next question is from an Autism Hangout listener with four children; two are neurotypical, one has ASD, one has PDD, and she's found herself pregnant. For this fifth child, she's wondering what the odds are of this child having ASD.

DR. TONY: From the information, it looks as though she has two out of four children on the spectrum. PDD-NOS means fragments of ASD: almost there, but not quite. The ratio is two out of four, so she's got a fifty-fifty chance as to what may happen with the next

child. This is something that's very important to pass on to people watching this video. Between 15 and 20 percent (roughly one in five) of the families have more than one person on the spectrum. What we tend to find is if that autism occurs in younger children, it tends to be stronger.

When the parents are marginally younger, the child may have a milder expression, such as Asperger's. If the subsequent child is on the spectrum, they are more likely to have classic autism. A boy, obviously, would have a greater likelihood, although the ratio of boys to girls is not four to one, but two to one.

So, what are the chances? You won't know until the child is about two years old. There are a variety of things that we look for at six months, nine months, a year, and beyond to monitor that child. I would firmly suggest there's probably a fifty-fifty chance.

CRAIG: Well, we wish you well. Good luck.

DR. TONY: Yes, and you may well come back with questions when the child is born about any significant thing you notice. One of the things we do check on is growth; one in four have a larger head circumference and seem to grow too rapidly from about three or four months of age. Not all, of course, but one of the signs that we look for early on is rapid acceleration, not only in height and length but also head circumference.

"What should we look for in a group home?"

CRAIG: "Dr. Tony, we have a son with Asperger's syndrome and we have been given the opportunity to assist our local county here in the United States in designing a group home for people on the spectrum. In your travels, have you run across what you feel is an example of an ideal home for young adults on the spectrum? Could you share the name of that home so we might be able to contact them for more information in the building of the home here in the US?"

DR. TONY: If you look at autism and Asperger's syndrome, there are many characteristics to account for. The first is the opportunity in that accommodation to have privacy and space—a single room—

Chapter Seventeen — Living with Autism

but also possibly a separate area for that individual (perhaps in their room) to watch television or take a little bit of food. If they need to, they've got their own enclave within that environment they can retreat to; it's a space where they can avoid social situations and enjoy being on their own.

The next part is related to group dynamics. Often a group of people are put together for political expediency, but consider checking first to see if they get along with each other. There's going to be group dynamics. If you have everyone at the same level, there's going to be lots of competition to see who does what. So, look for an equipped faculty that has a host of different functions that encourage working together as a unit. My view is that the decision on who lives there is based on their personalities rather than what's convenient for the administration.

Support and staff need to know about Asperger's syndrome, have some degree of training, and be consistent. Those with Asperger's don't like change—not only in routine, but change in people, as it takes them so long to get to know someone. My recommendation is that once you have the staff, they need to be trained and to be as consistent as possible to help these individuals.

The emphasis should be on that person learning greater independence skills. It may well be that they can then acquire skills they may not have had access to in the past. I also find that many with autism and Asperger's have quite difficult behavior during adolescence due to hormonal changes. If that person is past school age, it wouldn't necessarily be the end of their opportunities to learn. In fact, they may learn better because they are more calm and mature.

DR. TONY: I think the person with autism or Asperger's needs to be consulted about the decision so they feel that, in their agreement, they want to be successful. If they feel they had no choice, it may be very difficult to be successful.

Ask Dr. Tony

"Our son is struggling in a group home. What can we do?"

CRAIG: "Now that our Asperger's son is in a group home, he rarely comes out of his room, even to eat. Where he liked being social on occasion, he stays in his room now. He's getting his days and nights turned around and he rarely sees people. Once this situation happens, depression sets in. We've tried reasoning with him to come out, we've tried rewarding him when he does come out, and even gotten stern with him, but nothing works. What can we do to help him convince himself that he needs to get out and move more to keep himself on track?"

DR. TONY: Your son has discovered the cure for Asperger's syndrome: the ability to remove all the diagnostic criteria. You can't have a social disability in solitude. You don't have to worry about communication skills because you don't communicate with anybody, and you can do what you want to do (probably go on the computer) without anybody stopping you. As far as he's concerned, he's cured; he doesn't have to relate to others who torment him, tease him, or overwhelm him. He's king of his castle, and at the top of the tower is his bedroom.

He has no reason to go out, and if he goes out at night into the house there's hardly anybody around. He gets his food and then goes back in. I also suspect that he may have clinical depression in the sense that he has no energy or commitment to do the other things, and he's probably remembering the bullying and teasing that he is safe from in that environment. I think you need to talk to psychologists and psychiatrists about the possibility of clinical depression, medication, and cognitive behavior therapy, but getting him out of his room is not going to be easy.

Look at small steps for a reason to go out of his room. Perhaps he needs something for his computer, there's a purpose to get out. Through planned desensitization, he may gradually recognize that outdoor life is not as traumatic as it may have been in the past. He may also be encouraged through seeing your support. The problem is, if you don't do something now, it could last decades and his social and executive skills could deteriorate.

"I'm wondering if I'm bi-polar or have borderline personality disorder with my ASD. What would that look like?"

CRAIG: "I have post-traumatic stress disorder and I get depressed at times. Several people have suggested I may have a type of bipolar or borderline personality disorder on top of my ASD. What would that look like in a person with ASD? Whereas I enjoy solitude and find social situations exhausting, the women I know with BPD arc very engrossed in an emotional world that focuses around people and relationships, and they have an overwhelming fear of abandonment.

I can see where, superficially, some of the symptoms of BPD and ASD may appear similar, but the personal meaning and significance of these behaviors are really very different. How would I go about getting a clear diagnosis?"

DR. TONY: I see several women diagnosed or misdiagnosed with borderline personality disorder. They're not mutually exclusive. In borderline personality disorder, there can be an overreaction to an error and an intense depression attack occurs. Earlier, we described a rage attack. The same can occur with a depression attack, where the person with Asperger's may catastrophize an event.

It's part of the problem in emotion regulation where that negative emotion has a catastrophic overreaction that the person finds difficult to control. One of the aspects of borderline personality disorder is that the person is assumed to be, and can usually be, very good at reading facial expressions and body language and then misinterpreting people's intentions. The view with autism spectrum disorders is that they're not very good at reading body language. I will challenge that because my personal experience, clinically and in autobiographies, is that some with Asperger's have a sixth sense for sensing negative atmosphere. They don't do it by facial expressions or by a ton of words, but they just *feel* that something is wrong. They may use another channel to determine negative affect and then react accordingly.

There can be strong fears of rejection and abandonment in Asperger's because that has happened in their friendships. When their friendships end, they often say, "My friend was disloyal. I was a good friend, why did they abandon me and go to someone else?" There can be a history of that occurring with a person with Asperger's, and often women will react in a different way than men. Borderline personality disorder can occur in those with autism spectrum disorders, especially the women.

Chapter Seventeen — Living with Autism

"How can I locate autism-friendly schools?"

CRAIG: "Hi there. I just returned from a trip to the US, where I was visiting high schools who were willing to support my fifteen-year-old Asperger's son. He is currently mainstreamed in Singapore, but he's not enjoying his learning journey. The process in the US was made easier as I had an educational consultant who helped me find autism-friendly schools. Is there such a service in Australia? Otherwise, how else can I locate autism-friendly schools?"

DR. TONY: Good question. It's not restricted to Australia. I'm delighted that in the United States—it may be a particular state, unique to that state, or rare in other states—there's someone who will help you find a school. In Australia, we've developed for early intervention. Someone will guide the parents through the maze of early intervention strategies, but I don't know the equivalent of that in other countries.

What you tend to get is the unofficial "good school guide" organized by parents. Go on the Internet to see if you can locate the local parent support group and say, "Has anybody sent their child with ASD or Asperger's to this school?" You may have those who are graduates from or are currently at that school. You need a consumer's view. It's like buying a car; you want to talk to somebody who's driven that car. Schools have their protocol of what they're supposed to say. You want to know the reality of it, and that is what you get from parents.

Ask Dr. Tony

> **"My ten-year-old Aspie son inappropriately touched his younger brother. What can I do?"**

CRAIG: "How do I handle inappropriate touch? My ten-year-old Aspie boy has touched my four-year-old son inappropriately. The touch is sexual. I'm very concerned about his behavior, what can I do?"

DR. TONY: Don't panic. This is one intimate event, it does not mean that you've got somebody who is going to be a pervert in any way. This is a ten-year-old; however, those acts that he was involved with he's either experienced himself, seen in real life, or seen them on video. I'm afraid in our modern society those with ASD can have access to things which they're not able to understand. Unfortunately, the chances are he's seen or experienced something. It's best to find the source of that.

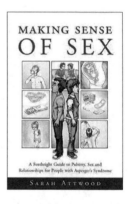

He may be exploring sensual or sexual experience as many pre-pubescent and pubescent people will do, but the ASD difference is that he doesn't know the conventions or the reactions of others: he doesn't know the script. This is an issue of ignorance, not perversion. He needs help to understand that there are certain things for kids, and there are certain things for adults. For example, having a baby is only done by parents for various reasons. Why is it that children can't have babies? Why is it that children can't drive a car? Why is it that children don't have a job? This is also why there are certain areas of touch and sensual experience that are not for children. Then explain, "How old are you? Ten. You're not an adult, it's not for you."

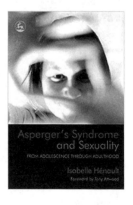

Chapter Seventeen — Living with Autism

You may use Carol Gray's *Comic-Strip Conversations* and draw an event with stick figures, speech, and thought bubbles to go through either the touching you're concerned about or how your son first got that knowledge. If you present your agitation, he's going to shut up. He's not going to tell you. You've got to say, "Look, I need to find out from my point of view. This is not a punishment. I just need to know what happened. Can you draw the situation when you first knew about this action? Can you then draw the action?"

Write questions in the thought bubbles such as, "How do you think the four-year-old was feeling when you did this? How do you think Mom was feeling? How do you think Dad was feeling?" He may be oblivious and need information. Stopping this now is logical because of the effect that it's going to have on various people, and also how other people will perceive you.

This is a great opportunity to promote a book called *Making Sense of Sex* by my wife, Sarah Attwood. It's written to introduce pre-pubescent and pubescent ASD individuals to sexuality. It's a book to be read by parents to help them explain the information; the issue here is that he's got information, but he doesn't know how to use it so he's using it inappropriately. He needs to understand the social conventions.

If professionals want to take it further, there's another book I'd recommend: *Asperger's Syndrome and Sexuality from Adolescence Through Adulthood* by Isabelle Henault. It gives you a program to work with the individual. Again, this is an issue of experience and ignorance, not perversion.

Ask Dr. Tony

"ASD and the legal system. Seek counsel that understands autism."

CRAIG: "I have a twenty-four-year-old sister that has been discriminated against because she's on the spectrum. In battling for her rights with the legal system, she has become very anxious. In a stressful ongoing situation like this, what can a loved one do to help them deal with the anxiety and give them support? Is there anything that the legal system can do to accommodate her special needs so she doesn't get misunderstood or brushed off?"

DR. TONY: The legal profession is one of the most conservative organizations you could possibly imagine. It will take them two to three decades to really recognize the characteristics of Asperger's syndrome. They may recognize it's an intellectual disability or psychiatric illness, but Asperger's is quite alien to them. Which is ironic, because I know several very successful judges and people in the legal profession with Asperger's syndrome. It's also a different culture, and those with Asperger's find it very difficult to adapt to new culture, language, and style. So, they have a double problem in this.

She may require legal representation that understands Asperger's syndrome and has a way of explaining it to a judge and the court as needed. As a clinician, I'm often involved with helping people give evidence. There could be issues of not understanding the nuances, the complex language, the culture, or even the sort of games that are played in court. Courts have nothing to do with justice and truth. It's a game, basically, and if you don't know the rules of the game, you're going to lose.

I think she needs someone who can help on two fronts: to explain the culture of the legal system almost as though she were in a foreign country (using Carol Gray's *Social Stories*™), and she's going to need legal representation that is aware of her confusion—especially if she is going to give evidence. The more agitated, concerned, and upset she is, the less coherent the information she will provide. They will need to have the ability to calm her down and support her.

I hope that she can continue, but often an approach in the legal system is a war of attrition where hopefully somebody collapses. However, from my clinical experience, people with Asperger's can keep going as a matter of principle. They can be very dogmatic and determined and need to be recognized as such.

Living with Autism
Gender Dysphoria

"What is gender dysphoria? Is it more prevalent in ASD?"

CRAIG: Here is a category that seems to be in the headlines these days as it relates to the autism community: gender dysphoria. "Is it possible for a male to have more of the typical female traits?" Could you give us a definition of the term *gender dysphoria*?

Ask Dr. Tony

DR. TONY: Gender dysphoria means you don't connect with the gender you were born as. It can lead to eventually undergoing medication and gender reassignment surgery. This is something that is only recently becoming recognized, and I'm getting more and more referrals.

There is a suggestion that almost half of those who are referred to a gender dysphoria clinic—many cities have those—have characteristics of ASD, often not diagnosed. It's a very interesting question: can the male have more of the "typical female" traits? Yes, in terms of not being macho, or being kind and considerate. These are not considered masculine traits, and they get their view of football players and rock stars and think, "That's not me. I'm a kind, nice person and associate with girls."

If they compare themselves with the stereotypical male, they won't connect with that. I strongly recommend that Aspie males be encouraged to recognize that masculinity is not exclusively macho. It can be a good parent who listens and is kind, considerate, and compassionate. These are not gendered conditions, they exist in both males and females.

They need to know and hear from other males that masculinity has a very broad sense and includes being a caring, compassionate person. It's not the exclusive preserve of females. It may be the case that a boy with Asperger's has always found other boys dismissive, bullying, and teasing, but he has found girls to be kind and to have lots of friends. This can cause beliefs like, "I want friends and a good social network. If I became female, I would have friends." It would be a cure for autism.

Another component that can occur is feeling isolated. In adolescence, many go through an awakening of sexuality and may discover a whole range of information on the Internet. They don't get that information from their peer group because they don't have many friends, if any. The Internet will give them a long list of descriptions that they may find interesting.

Then, they may be welcomed and encouraged in a particular expression of sexuality, which is very tempting and enjoyable. They want to have a new family, so they seek out a new culture of isolated, marginalized people. It can be very tempting to have a group who are keen to know them and explore their abilities.

This can also occur with recruitment for extremist political groups. The Aspie person starts to think this could be of benefit to them, and if they're not careful, it becomes a special interest. There's phenomenal knowledge and expertise that's acquired, along with the determination of a single-minded characteristic. Now, there's supposed to be counselling and time to consider this, but Aspies make their decision and leave their parents wondering, "Where did this come from?"

There's another group in ASD who have felt they're the wrong gender, often from preschool years. Girls with Asperger's may have found boys simpler, easier to get along with, and very practical in what they do. They become a tomboy. They may despise femininity, and become quite concerned when they go through puberty that they're feminized and they don't want to be.

One of the pathways to anorexia is to maintain an androgynous physique. The view for the girl may be, "I feel like the boys, would my life be dramatically changed and improved if I became a boy?" Sometimes, these characteristics have been there for many years. When looking at gender dysphoria, this is a major life-changing decision that must be taken very carefully.

One of the characteristics I look for, as a clinician, is what's underneath: the person is saying, "I don't like who I am." When I work with the person, I say, "Whether you're male or female, I'm not concerned about that. I want you to have a positive sense of self, whatever your gender may be." That's the area that I work on.

CRAIG: Are there any books forthcoming? Is there any more research coming out?

DR. TONY: It's just started to emerge. Win Lawson has transitioned from female to male. He is a friend of mine. I saw Win at a conference a few weeks ago and he now has a beard, strong arms, and so on. It was fascinating because his daughter was there and she shouted out, "Mom!" Of course, this very male character turned around to her.

No, there isn't literature yet. The gender dysphoria clinics are screening people for ASD, and this is a major pathway. We must wonder, are they genuine or not? Is it a special interest that has an expiration date?

When I follow those who had the transition, some say, "Yes, it's been what I wanted. I'm happy," but a significant proportion will say, "My problems are still here."

Chapter Seventeen — Living with Autism

"Being ASD and a transgender, will I have a second puberty?"

CRAIG: This is a two-part question. "I've met many transgender people who also have autism, especially female to male. Why is that? Can my autism symptoms change through my second puberty (after the operation)?"

DR. TONY: Yes, I have met several people who have changed gender and have an autism spectrum disorder. I think there are two components here: one is neurological and the other is psychological. There is a suggestion that many girls with Asperger's syndrome seem to be more inclined to be friends with boys and to be a tomboy as a child. They like boys' toys and think, "I get their jokes, I enjoy being with the boys, I'm also interested in mathematics and engineering, and I don't like fashion." There can be what we call the "male brain" in a neurological sense; the person really does feel an affinity to being male and may decide to pursue that through surgery. That may be rather drastic, but it can be done.

From a psychological standpoint, they are basically saying, "I don't like who I am, and if I change gender, will I change my personality and possibly cure myself of Asperger's syndrome?" For example, some of the boys will say, "The boys bully and tease me, but the girls are nice and kind and they've got lots of friends. If I became a girl, then maybe I would have the kindness that they have." What may occur psychologically is, "I don't like who I am and I want to change gender." I tend to find that when those who've had the gender reassignment surgery realize it hasn't changed ASD characteristics, they are still the same physiologically. They may have changed gender, but the issues of understanding facial expressions, reading body language, and making friends remain. It may help in some ways.

Ask Dr. Tony

"Why is 'closure' so important to someone with Asperger's?"

CRAIG: "I want to hear more about the trouble that we Aspies have with closure."

DR. TONY: In terms of closure in processing or working on a particular topic, it's almost like the Asperger's mindset is calibrated and adjusted to solve the problem. If a task must be stopped before it's completed, the person has great difficulty switching to a new mindset due to the need for closure. Once completed, the person can then move on to something else.

In a job that's great, because they'll be there at eleven o'clock at night making everything perfect, but you can't do that at school. You've got to be flexible, especially in high school. It also means that the person must have a full level of understanding. Otherwise, their mindset will become so focused that they can't do anything else. That's one of the reasons for closure. Sometimes what I'll do is say, "On the old-fashioned video machines you have a pause button, and we're going to need to pause." It means that there needs to be a transition of solitude or physical activity between the two activities. You've got a clean whiteboard for the next activity.

"Do gluten-free and dairy-free diets help behavior issues? What about supplements?"

CRAIG: The next two questions have to do with diet. "Dr. Tony, I've been down the path of gluten- and dairy-free diets, as well as biomedical intervention with supplements like zinc. Does diet help behavior in children with Asperger's?"

DR. TONY: I think it does warrant investigation. It doesn't cure, but it may help the individual. We are identifying metabolic disorders as a risk for autoimmune disorders in the autism population. This tends to be done by parents and people in an entrepreneurial way rather than scientifically. I do know some families that have found gluten- or casein-free diets successful, which is great! For others, however, it has made no difference. I wouldn't worry, but I will urge some degree of caution.

CRAIG: The next question is, "I'm wondering how to know if a gluten-free/casein-free diet is right for my son. He had a yeast infection in his stomach at two months, which was followed by projectile vomiting for the first half of his life. Presently, he has no signs of intestinal pain, but he does have strange issues with food and eating. The reason I'm asking is because it appears that a lot of children with autism throw tantrums and have certain behavior problems due to digestion. I want to know if an endoscopy would be appropriate to check for abnormalities."

DR. TONY: It can be an issue of the sensory quality of the food. That's a separate issue. Gastrointestinal digestion problems do occur in ASD, but they also occur in other developmental disorders. If you're concerned about it as a parent, I would go to the gastroenterologist for advice. Whether an endoscopy would help with a medical decision will be based on the clinical description that you have. I think, for peace of mind, you would probably want to do it just in case there is something that should be dealt with. That determination I pass on to medical colleagues (the gastroenterologist) on an individual case-by-case basis.

Ask Dr. Tony

> **"Does the gluten-free/casein-free diet work?"**

CRAIG: "The gluten-free/casein-free diet has been out there for a while and has a lot of advocates saying it really works. The government and other testing agencies are saying it doesn't. What has been your experience with this diet?"

DR. TONY: What the government may be saying is that overall in a large population, it does not make a huge difference. However, it might make a significant difference for certain individuals. Within their huge sample of several thousand or so, there may be some where it did work, but that's camouflaged amongst those where it didn't. There's a simple biological test that can be undergone to determine whether it will work for you. You won't know until you try it.

My view is give it a try. It won't do you any harm, so be sensible about it. Talk to a dietitian beforehand to see if there's anything that may be missing from that diet. I believe here we're dealing with an adult, twenty years old. The advantage with an adult is you can explain why you're doing it. When you're with a kid, four or five years old, they can't understand why they can't have the same food that everyone else is having at the meal table. Sometimes, the whole family is going to go on the same diet or else the kids ask, "Why can't I have bread? Why can't I have that milk with my cereal?"

I think you need to have a look at it and see if you do benefit from it. You won't know until you try it. I don't think you're going to do any harm in giving it a try.

Chapter Seventeen — Living with Autism

"Why do so many UK children have mental health issues today?"

CRAIG: The next question is from England. It starts with this statement: "A National Autistic Society campaign has just revealed that 70 percent of the children here in the UK have a mental health problem. Forty percent have two mental health issues, and some of these children are as young as five years old. The NAS campaign is calling for professionals to be correctly trained so they can understand these children and not make their mental health conditions worse. While I completely agree with this campaign, surely we need to find out why so many children are having these problems."

DR. TONY: We now recognize that there are constitutional, neurological reasons why those with autism spectrum disorders are prone to mental health issues, predominantly anxiety. Constitutionally, they are natural worriers. They find it very hard not to catastrophize, panic, and worry about what's going to occur. This happens for a variety of reasons, including low self-esteem, bullying, teasing, and feeling different than other kids. Depression is likely to occur.

There may be mental health issues in terms of frustration due to not knowing what else to do to solve a problem. Major issues in a different profile of learning leads them to become quite explosive. In other words, the experience and expression of emotions is a major problem for such individuals and is not simply caused by environment. However, the environment can make it worse. From my own experience as a clinical psychologist, psychiatric hospitals and clinics do more harm than good for those with autism and Asperger's.

I have never known someone with autism or Asperger's who has ever benefitted from placement in a psychiatric hospital. Never. It has made them worse. From my point of view, there are constitutional reasons. People need to understand the challenges that are faced by such individuals, that they will not be solved simply by taking medication. Medication will not give you friends. Medication will not improve your self-esteem. Medication will not give you new ideas of how to solve a problem or to stop the frustration. It's not an issue of just medicating such individuals, it's analyzing their circumstances, quality of life, coping strategies, and developing skills.

I think all children with high-functioning autism or Asperger's should have, from kindergarten to graduating from high school, at least one hour a week studying emotions in school. From very young children—four or five years old—learning about expressing happiness and sadness, to teenagers learning about jealousy, love, embarrassment, and so on. Somebody should guide them in the vocabulary and the expression using drama or similar activities so they become fluent in understanding emotions. Eventually, when they have emotional problems, they can articulate them. There should be people who can listen to and help them deal with those problems.

Chapter Seventeen — Living with Autism

CRAIG: "Does Asperger's with a seemingly genetic component pick up momentum through each generation? Should future generations in a family be made aware, just as much as with any other type of genetic disorder or condition? We are undiagnosed but there is a family pattern. I'm concerned the next generations will not understand ASD."

DR. TONY: Yes, the geneticists say that certain characteristics can become greater through the generations, but it's also a question of who your partner is. Sometimes there's an attraction from Aspie to Aspie, but also extreme neurotypical to an Aspie, and that extreme neurotypical may have ASD in their family history, too. You're combining two families, and those characteristics will be accentuated. You'll have more extreme neurotypicals and more Aspies.

If it were increasing through generations, what would you do? If the geneticist informed you there's a strong probability your child will have an autism spectrum disorder, what would you do about that? If we eliminated those with Asperger's, we'd lose Mozart, Bill Gates, Einstein, and many others.

It's better to understand the individual, not to remove them from the human gene pool. I do agree that I have found families where the ASD seems to get greater through the generations. However, we are more sensitive today, whereas years ago people could create an isolated lifestyle—in a monastery, for example, or at school. They just sat at a desk and learned; they didn't work as a group, and there was no concept of teamwork. Aspies were always here!

Ask Dr. Tony

> ## "Is it harder for Asperger's kids to learn a foreign language?"

CRAIG: "My daughter is sixteen and has Asperger's syndrome. Most colleges want kids to have a foreign language in high school. Is it harder for an AS kid to learn to use a foreign language out of context?"

DR. TONY: Those with autism and Asperger's already speak a second language: the social language. They're already bilingual, or bilingual-bicultural, because they're living in both neurotypical and Aspie cultures. When it comes to Asperger's and language, I tend to find that if they're good, they speak the language they're learning *exactly* as they hear it—without having the accent of their home country. They will speak and a native will mistake them as being native, too. They could also be hopeless at it; if they are, cut it out and don't do it. If your daughter is good at it, superb, she'll be multilingual! I have met many such individuals in my travels to international conferences. If she's not good at it or doesn't like it, it causes more problems than it's worth. If in doubt, cut it out.

Chapter Seventeen — Living with Autism

"Asperger's faulty logic."

CRAIG: This person has an older brother who's forty-two and has Asperger's syndrome. Their mother passed away, she and her older brother get along well, but her brother's wife doesn't get along with her. The older brother accused her of possibly poisoning their mother. She was obviously upset by this. She didn't really understand where it came from, but she assumed it must have come from his wife. She really wants to get along with her brother.

Her question is, "Does his Asperger's mean I have to do everything the way he wants to do it or interpret the things the way he says? Why is my relationship with my older brother now always one way? There doesn't seem to be any empathy or compassion or give-and-take on his behalf. Is he likely to change his view in the future?" She wants to know how to deal with him in this most unpleasant situation.

DR. TONY: In relation to the accusation that she may have poisoned their mother, I call this "Aspie faulty logic." He may have overheard something and misinterpreted it, or misunderstood what was occurring and made as assumption that has now become categorical. She needs to ask her brother, "When did you first have that thought? What were the circumstances? Who said what?" Sometimes people make passing statements like, "Oh, I bet you killed your mother for the inheritance." The person was joking, of course, but an Aspie may think that's a serious accusation.

Regarding her relationship with her brother, it's going to be a difficult one because he has his own way of doing things. At forty-two, he's fairly stable in his personality and ways. Try to work with him on a balanced compromise between the two of you. Usually, in those situations we primarily go through the Aspie's perspective and acknowledge the way things look from their point of view. I'd say, "Well, here is my perspective. We need to compromise and sort things out, otherwise we'll be in conflict, disappointment, and annoyance. To avoid those emotions, we need to work constructively on this, be honest, and compromise."

Do this without emotional accusations, because once you become emotional with him he may become defensive or antagonistic. Work logically. Sometimes it helps if there's a third party, like a family member, that can act as a neutral person to understand both perspectives. There is a risk: if the person with Asperger's decides they dislike a family member, they may never talk to them again. There can be a very black-and-white tolerance or intolerance of people.

CRAIG: Approach it logically, pragmatically, not emotionally, and if there's a third party there that her brother trusts, that's best. But not the brother's wife.

DR. TONY: No. It needs to be somebody neutral who understands both perspectives. It may be a family friend.

"The value of carrying an 'I have autism—what to do for me' card."

CRAIG: "How does someone with Asperger's and anxiety learn to cope in situations where someone may or may not be aware of autism and Asperger's? What can they do to help save the situation so they don't get incarcerated or they don't suffer violence?"

When people have Asperger's, they are often misinterpreted, we all know that. But sometimes this misinterpretation can get violent to where police will put handcuffs on the person with Asperger's syndrome because either they were not answering questions, or they were acting strangely.

Chapter Seventeen — Living with Autism

DR. TONY: The incarceration can also be in a psychiatric unit, it doesn't have to be in a jail. Sometimes the police will recognize the person is unusual and they'll refer them to psychiatric services. For a person with Asperger's dealing with intense emotion, the coherence of speaking, the clarity of thought, and the ability to explain themselves is gone. I recommend the person carries something with them similar to a diabetes alert that an emergency crew can look at and adjust their treatment.

This person should have a series of cards in their pocket that describes themselves and Asperger's. "You may feel that I am being psychotic, you may think that I am being irrational, you may be actually scared by my behavior, but I have Asperger's syndrome. This means I'm misinterpreting your body language, I'm not very good at understanding how to deal with officials. What I need is solitude. The worst thing to do is to try and restrain me. I need time to calm down, I will then be able to explain. You need not to be angry with me but be supportive. I don't seek compassion, I seek concern and solitude."

If the Aspie individual finds themselves unable to speak, they can hand the card to them. It should contain a rational explanation of your situation, and information including a secondary phone number: "If in doubt, contact this number to reach a relative/friend who can give more information." To ask the person with Asperger's to suddenly create a persona or ability to translate what they are doing in those intense moments is not possible. If the information is on a card, it can take some of the pressure off and make the situation easier for everyone involved.

The person reading the card can then handle the situation correctly.

Ask Dr. Tony

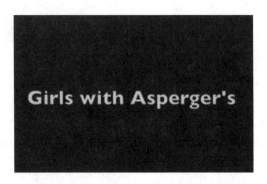

Identifying Girls with Autism: Part One

CRAIG: Dr. Tony, globally, the statistics are that for every four boys that are born with autism, there's one girl. Is this observation still accurate?

DR. TONY: No, I don't think it is. When it comes to Asperger's syndrome, we find that girls are very good at camouflaging their social confusion, hiding in a group, and making sure they don't get noticed. If you look very carefully, I think the ratio is actually about two to one.

CRAIG: Interesting. Is that based on your observations in Australia, or globally?

DR. TONY: Globally. We're noticing that in the clinic we have here in Brisbane, the adult group's ratio is about two to one. These are women who, with maturity, have recognized that they've always been different and finally had the confidence to go and check this out. Or they've had a child themselves with autism and Asperger's syndrome. I think from that alternative pathway; the ratio is probably about two to one.

Chapter Seventeen — Living with Autism

CRAIG: This next question comes from Rudy Simone. Now, Rudy is the author of *22 Things a Woman Must Know if She's in Love with a Man with Asperger's Syndrome* and also *Asperger's in the Workplace*. Rudy herself is a person on the spectrum. Her question is, "Is there any special training today that's being provided to psychologists, psychiatrists, and doctors to help them recognize AS in women—which so often goes un-diagnosed?"

DR. TONY: First of all, a message to Rudy that her book *22 Things a Woman Must Know if She's in Love with a Man with Asperger's Syndrome* is excellent!

Regarding actual training, very little is done for girls and women with Asperger's syndrome. I nearly always have a section on it in my presentations so that those in the audience see illustrated components for girls with Asperger's. When we look at the various ways that girls may be diagnosed, it may not be until they're in their teenage years that they're identified.

Sometimes the diagnosis starts with a secondary disorder such as anorexia nervosa, depression, or obsessive-compulsive disorder. When a full developmental history is taken, we recognize that there is indeed Asperger's syndrome, but it may not be until they're in their teens or early twenties and encountering difficulties with relationships that we identify them. The professionals seeing them may not necessarily be professionals in autism and Asperger's syndrome.

A few weeks ago, Michelle Garnett and I conducted a workshop over two days specifically for girls and women with Asperger's syndrome here in Brisbane. The most important parts of the presentation were the descriptions by women with Asperger's syndrome of their childhood and how they hid in various groups to avoid being bullied, teased, and tormented. Being hidden, they never came to the attention of the authorities. That workshop went down extremely well and I'm hoping to hold them in the USA and other countries in the future. Watch for a one-day workshop specifically on girls and women with Asperger's syndrome!

"How can I best help my school-age girl with autism?"

CRAIG: "From your experience, what should parents focus on for their school-age girls to become productive adults and a part of the community?" This question is from Ann Milan, the author of *Autism-Believe in the Future: From Infancy to Independence.*

DR. TONY: For school-age girls, one of the difficulties is going to be the bullying and teasing from other girls, which can be horrendous for self-esteem. There can be issues with fashion, makeup, and boyfriend/girlfriend relationships; the social world of girls is far more intense than boys, and if you're confused in that environment it's going to affect your self-esteem and self-identity in quite tragic ways. My concern is that we need to work with the peer group to identify one or two girls who may be supportive.

One of the things I found is that sometimes the girl with Asperger's can only have one friend at a time. That's all they can cope with. That friend can provide guidance, support, and protection from some of the predators. My view is, we need to work with the peer group for acceptance and use a buddy system.

> **"How can school-age girls with autism develop better friendships?"**

CRAIG: That segues nicely into this next question. "How can girls with Asperger's syndrome develop better friendships?"

DR. TONY: I think they need to learn how, but most of the social skills groups and activities are for boys. When we had social skills groups in the past, the girls were in a minority and felt as such. I think they really need an opportunity to meet and make friends with other girls with Asperger's syndrome, because they understand each other and also to have someone who can provide the guidance they need in a professional capacity. At our Minds and Hearts Clinic, we've now started girls' groups that specifically focus on the issues they face at elementary, junior high, and high school.

CRAIG: Are these groups initially pulled together as social groups, or are they more academic groups?

DR. TONY: They're social groups to help girls understand friend-ships and to address issues of self-esteem. In part, we focus on what-ever the participants in the group want to focus on. Each group is unique and composed of unique individuals. We can't determine exactly what we're going to go through. So, what we tend to do is say, "Okay guys, what are your issues and problems, what can we do to help?"

CRAIG: Are the parents instrumental in organizing these group functions as well?

DR. TONY: Yes. My colleagues organize them and if they're going to be successful, it needs to be information that's passed on to par-ents, and subsequently to schools. The girls are prone to become very introspective: they may either become depressed or escape into imagination. Because they're no trouble—often absorbed in their imagination or their books—they're often overlooked.

"How are women with Asperger's fitting into the employment arena?"

CRAIG: "How are women with Asperger's fitting into the employ-ment arena?"

DR. TONY: Marvelously! There are some jobs that are more likely for girls or women with Asperger's. Those can range from librari-anship to teaching in special education and early childhood. They could be exceptionally talented in that area, but I also know several women with Asperger's syndrome who have been very determined to become counselors, either social workers or psychologists. In that position, they can explore Asperger's syndrome as counselors to members of their own culture, helping them in a variety of ways. I think it's a great idea for women to earn degrees in the caring professions and then become a specialist in Asperger's.

CRAIG: That's a wonderful suggestion!

"How can I better communicate with a non-verbal ASD person?"

CRAIG: "I help run a social group for adults on the spectrum with an age range of eighteen to twenty-six. My goal is to help everyone get the most out of our time together. We have a variety of participants. However, I'm greatly concerned about those with limited ability to verbalize their thoughts. Recently, a completely non-verbal participant joined us. I have a difficult time knowing what he wants and needs and I don't want to seem condescending. How can I meaningfully include and communicate with these participants?"

DR. TONY: It's very important to approach that person with respect. You can't look at the lack of speech as an indication of intellectual ability, as there can be movement disturbances as to why they can't get their brain to communicate with their mouth. They certainly will be sensitive to integrity. It's always difficult to know how much that person understands, but I think in this case you might consider contacting the parents to identify the "mannerisms that have a message." That is, if he has classic autism, he may have little flaps and movements, rocking ... mannerisms that are a message. I look for what I call a "foreign phrase dictionary." Sometimes parents can videotape this so that you reference it for signals that mean "I'm happy and I agree," and the signals that mean "I'm upset." Then you are able to interpret.

That means when you're making a suggestion—for example, "Should we go to the shopping mall?"—ask the person to think about it and respond using their body language. You can gauge the person's reaction by reading unique body language which is a signature for that individual.

CRAIG: Very good. A lot of "yes" and "no" questions could be appropriately responded to by this individual.

DR. TONY: Indeed. It takes time, but it's worth it.

"Do ASD characteristic get worse with age?"

CRAIG: "Is it possible that some problems get worse as the person with ASD gets older? I find more alone time is now needed for recovery. I'm experiencing feelings and emotions no longer in just shades of gray. It seems that I'm only getting along well with animals, and no longer have an ability to get along with humans."

DR. TONY: There are two components to this. As you age, the parts of the brain that seem to go first are the frontal lobes: the thinking and planning part of the brain. That's the part of the brain that those with Asperger's need to process social information. To plan what to do socially and read the information are intellectual exercises, not intuitive.

As the aging process leads to frontal lobe decay, there will be less ability to socialize without being exhausted and you'll find your intellectual capacity and concentration has lessened. You may steer towards familiar areas that are not too stressful for you.

There's another component. I'm supervising a PhD student doing her research on aging, and she's been interviewing many people with Asperger's along with their partners. There seems to be a higher-than-expected reaction of becoming calmer and more accepting in aging years. Some of the Aspie features can diminish in the later stages of life. I was not expecting this but what is overwhelming in the research is that the sense of maturity may be softening some features. Whether this is psychological, maturing, or frontal lobe issues is what we'll continue looking at.

Living with Autism
Do ASD Issues Get Worse With Age?

"Tips for how someone with ASD can better express feelings."

CRAIG: This young person is saying, "It drives me nuts. My mother is always saying 'answer the question' and I think I am! I'm so frustrated and upset I just can't stand it anymore. What does she want from me? Then I get asked, 'How are you feeling?' and 'Why do you do that?' What am I supposed to do? Because I don't have a clue!"

DR. TONY: I like this one. This perfectly describes an ASD characteristic: trouble converting thought and emotion to speech. "Why did you do that?" "I don't know." "What are you feeling now?" "I don't know." However, I have found that those with ASD can be incredibly eloquent in describing their thoughts and feelings using other avenues.

They can send you an email, write you a story, find a piece of music that describes their thoughts and feelings, or find a scene in one of their favorite shows or movies. They can search for images online and choose one that represents the feeling. Try something other than verbal communication.

The person with ASD is not being stubborn, and the parents need to know it's a genuine difficulty converting thought and emotion to speech. He needs encouragement, processing time, or an alternative means of communication.

"How do I get people to listen to me?"

CRAIG: "How do I get people to listen to me? I'm thirty-six now, and I'm finding out there's no help for someone my age with my issues. I see everything like a picture, full of colors and shapes, and sounds are so overwhelming. It's so bad that I start having panic attacks as soon as I go outside. I never could keep a job or a relationship and I blank out multiple times a day. I get tired and no one has figured out the pain in my legs, which is bad enough that I can't walk up stairs.

"I also have food issues and energy problems. I used to make sounds and rock in a corner. I've been told to get over it, 'you look fine' or 'why can't you just be like this person?' How can someone my age finally get help, or at least listened to?"

Chapter Seventeen — Living with Autism

DR. TONY: I think you need to be listened to, understood, and appreciated for what you're going through. When neurotypicals don't understand, their view is simply, "Don't think about it. Just move on. You'll get over it," because they've never experienced it. What you're is describing is sensory overload stress in many ways, and stress can lead to a breakdown of the immune system and general health.

You need a physician who is experienced in ASD to give some guidance over what is reasonable for you, and for people to listen to you—because this is a cry for help. It's not indolence, it's not laziness. If it were that simple, it would have been addressed years ago.

You need some degree of understanding and encouragement to cope with the stress, but also to significantly reduce the stress in your life. A very good physical workup is needed to find out if there's something going on in the autoimmune disorders.

"ASD and addiction."

CRAIG: "My seventeen-year-old has turned to drugs, what can I do? He was put out of the adolescent psychiatric unit and onto the street two hours away from his home with no phone, no money, and not even a bus ticket. He seems to be in the 'too hard' basket. He's had several hospital admissions, but all this does is make him more angry. Where can he go for help?"

DR. TONY: I have to express my personal issues here; my son has Asperger's syndrome and he's been a drug addict now for nearly twenty years. Obviously, I've talked with him about the issue of addiction. There are several reasons why it begins. One is to engage or disengage from reality. To engage, one can try to be relaxed in social situations using alcohol and marijuana. When someone is relaxed, he or she can participate more freely and engage with the marginalized group who are pleased to see them join in their culture.

It can also be used to disengage and create a bubble of detachment to self-medicate—for anxiety, in particular. Unfortunately, the Alcohol and Drug Dependency Services aren't sufficiently knowledgeable about ASD, which is ironic because there's a suggestion that about one in four of those in Alcohol and Drug Dependency Services have characteristics of ASD. They are notorious for not responding to group therapy, disclosure of thoughts and feelings relating to the others, and all those neurotypical therapies are not designed for Aspies.

My son has been to rehab many times. He's also been to prison and he said, "Dad, at least in prison I had my own cell. I had my own solitude. In rehab, I had to share a dormitory with sixteen men. I had no privacy. The staff there didn't seem to understand me, didn't seem to realize the difficulties I have in disclosing and talking about my feelings."

He left with the intention of never returning. The difficulty with this seventeen-year-old is if he decides that they don't understand him, then he's going to have to have a recovery on his own.

I wrote the foreword in a book called *Drinking, Drug Use and Addiction in the Autism Community* by Elizabeth Kunreuther and Ann Palmer. It's been published in the last few months as a description of the issues of addiction and Asperger's. I think that should be essential reading for all those in this area. What I would like to see are mentors with Asperger's who have been through addiction. I'm hoping my son will eventually talk about the challenges and different ways of coping, because taking drugs can be a lethal activity. He's been near death many times.

As a parent, you are worried because you can't get through to them. But that's what they want. It's isolation. As a father, I have not been able to get through to my son because there's a wall of intoxication with a variety of drugs.

I feel for this person. They need to do something soon, in terms of possibly finding a one-on-one therapy based on ASD. We're developing that as much as we can but at this stage, I do not have anything other than this one book that may help.

> **"I'm codependent on my parents but want to be independent. What can I do?"**

CRAIG: "I came across the term 'codependent relationship' a while ago and I believe that describes the sort of relationship that I now have with my parents. I desperately want to get out of it with as little damage to my family as possible. I have the usual Aspie problems with very few friends, and so there is no one to take over the job. I absolutely need my parents' help but I don't want them making decisions for me and taking control of my life. Is there any advice you can give me on how to improve our relationship to ensure my independence in the long-term?"

DR. TONY: This is another good one. There are several elements to this. Usually, the person with Asperger's has problems with daily living skills, from doing up their buttons, to riding a bike, managing their budgets, or organizing their daily schedule. Due to the lack of executive function (planning, organizing, time management components—especially in high school), parents have realized it's quicker and more efficient if they do it instead.

That sets up a dependency where Mom or Dad says, "Well, I'll do it for you." They know that it works, but they've got to back off. They found that it makes everyone's life easier if they do your budgeting, sort out your plans for today, and so on, but that's maintaining dependency. I have to work with parents, especially with adolescents and young adults, and say, "Back up. If he makes a mistake, he's going to learn from his own experiences. He doesn't really learn by watching others. He's got to do it himself. Now, that means he's got the dignity of risk, and sometimes he's going to fail, but he'll learn from it. You can't put him in bubble wrap all his life."

In the long-term, one day for his own self-esteem and independence, the parents will have to hand over the reins.

Sometimes it may be a very maternal, caring parent who enjoys this role and wants to be needed. There's a dynamic between two parties that requires a third party to say, "Look, he needs to learn by himself. You can be a good parent by letting him learn from his own experiences and become more independent, even if he makes a mistake." In a way, the parents are coveting him and supporting him, but this will protect the parents as much as the child.

CRAIG: You would suggest a third party enters the scene to set some boundaries between the parents and son?

DR. TONY: Yes. Someone needs to be objective and reassuring, there's an enormous amount of anxiety and antagonism.

Ask Dr. Tony

Bonus Sections

Bonus Sections

Answers to the Most Common Questions about Autism

Contained in these five question categories are portions of the 140 questions that comprise the bulk of this book.

CRAIG: Dr. Tony, over the years you've been asked lots of questions about autism from people all around the world. What would be the five most common questions?

DR. TONY: I think the first one almost always involves the issues of diagnosis: how to diagnose, who can do it, how reliable the diagnosis is, which instruments should be used, and what the barriers to a diagnosis are, especially for adults.

1. Issues of Diagnosis:

The first point to make is that diagnosis is not an exact science, it's a matter of opinion. Different clinicians may notice different characteristics. However, we're all looking for patterns.

There are instruments that are accurate at identifying ASD—especially ASD in its severe form, classic autism. For ASD level one, formerly known as Asperger's, they're not quite as effective because the characteristics we are looking for are very subtle. The more experienced the clinician, the more accurate the diagnosis, especially for the girls and women with Asperger's.

Recognizing and identifying characteristics in one's developmental history is very important. As such, clinical experience is far more powerful in confirming a diagnosis than the score on a particular instrument or test.

The good news is, often when a diagnosis does occur this means one can now have closure on the past. You can start to look at your strengths and make plans based on who you really are.

2. Emotion Management:

The second most common question is about the management of emotions. Meltdowns and constant anxiety can be much more debilitating than the characteristics of Asperger's themselves. When it comes to emotion management, we have some strong strategies and tools. For instance, anxiety and depression can be successfully addressed through anger management.

You could have what I call "ASD pure." That is a problem in understanding what someone is thinking and feeling, social convention, sensory sensitivity, and so on. However, with ASD comes the risk of developing a mood disorder. We have no idea why but there may be something constitutional or genetic that leads a person to be somewhere on a continuum from an optimistic, enduring natural warrior to a person both discouraged and pessimistic. Being the latter could lead to an anxiety disorder or depression.

When I talk to adults with ASD I ask, "What are your biggest challenges in life?" They often say managing anxiety, coping with depression, or managing their temper at times. The good

news here is that we now have a range of approaches that can successfully be used for these conditions. Anxiety is easier to treat than depression. If the person is just feeling sad or down, we can achieve better moods; however, severe depression is not easily alleviated.

CRAIG: That's great news! It's interesting to know that when we did the research for *Been There. Done That. Try This!* we found anxiety is the number one issue that comes up as one of the most stressful, pressing issues in the life of somebody with Asperger's. Depression is number five.

3. ASD in Girls and Women:

The third question would be about the expression of ASD in girls and women. For many women with Asperger's syndrome, they often think, "Where do I fit in? What is my role? I've always felt different but I don't know quite where I belong."

A characteristic of ASD is to try and find patterns. Women can adeptly observe people to discover patterns of life. As they observe from a distance, in identifying and copying the pattern they pick up cues of what to do.

Girls and women can also be quite good at camouflaging: not being identified for who they really are. Many learn from observing a situation, analyzing what's taking place, imitating ("faking") the actions of others, thereby camouflaging themselves in the process. We're now realizing it's not specific to just girls. Boys can do it, too. My son who has Asperger's syndrome did just that. He was so good at "faking it" that his diagnosis was delayed by a matter of years.

Women can be very successful with this technique, but as with my son it can delay a diagnosis and problems continue. For example, the person may cope very well at school, but it's emotionally exhausting! They're using their intellect to socialize rather than learn the lessons being taught by teachers. So, when they get home they're either absolutely spent or have suppressed their feelings to the point where they become explosive.

Maja Toudal – The AnMish on Youtube

Once diagnosed, I encourage all to be what I call "a first-rate Aspie" versus a "second-rate neurotypical." Be true to who you are. Yes, life is a stage. When you are in the company of others, you may have to act. I recognize the people with Asperger's who do act should get an Oscar every day for their performance as a neurotypical. It's exhausting! That comment comes from Maja Toudal, who has Asperger's, and has been a great tutor to me in this area.

4. School Issues:

A lot of questions I get relate to school issues, such as how ASD students learn best, how to get along with others (teamwork), dealing with bullying and teasing, and making and keeping friends.

School is taught in a social, conversational context. Social conversation is not the Aspie way of learning. The Aspie way of learning is in solitude, usually looking at a screen or reading a book. In a classroom environment, they are often underachieving, overwhelmed, and confused. What a teacher needs to do is translate the curriculum into an Aspie's style of learning—"Aspergerese"—and that can lead to more success.

School also promotes learning through teamwork. Kids with ASD know very clearly, "I'm different. I'm not cool. I don't fit in." What's often worse is the bullying and teasing that can occur.

That can have profound effects in terms of lower self-esteem and depression. Again, teachers need to step in and help. Sometimes parents have to be the ones to help teachers learn how ASD kids learn best!

5. Employment and Adult Relationships:

A fifth area of questions would be around the adult issues of employment and relationships. I'm frequently asked questions about how to get and keep a job, as well as coping with office politics and managers. Sometimes, someone with ASD will tell me they'd rather do tasks their own way, rather than the way the company asked them to do it. It's not just getting a job that's important, it's staying employed. In the book *Been There. Done That. Try This!*, we learned through first-hand stories from Aspies in the workplace how they dealt with such situations. There are also some practical answers in this book on how you might approach similar situations. The good news is that the workplace is now identifying the gifts of Asperger's and seeking their unique skill sets. So don't be discouraged! If you haven't yet found a job, keep looking.

The other area is relationships: "How do I get a partner and how do I relate to a partner? How can I understand and cope with a neurotypical partner and the challenges that they face?" People on the spectrum want to learn about romance, love, and how to navigate a long-term relationship. These are all common themes. Counselors, psychologists, and romanticists around the world are all working on these questions ... and succeeding, as are marriages involving people on the spectrum. For answers to these intriguing issues, I invite you all to "stay tuned!"

Ask Dr. Tony

For over two decades, Dr. Tony Attwood has been a frequent speaker at autism conferences worldwide. His audiences are parents, authors, medical professionals and researchers, speakers, therapists and counselors, teachers, social workers, community/public servants, people living with autism, and more. Dr. Attwood has been asked tens of thousands of questions. Here are his answers to lists of those asked most frequently, by specific audience:

- Five frequent questions from parents
- Five frequent questions from teachers
- Five frequent questions from public servants (i.e. police, firemen)
- Five frequent questions from social workers

Top Five Questions from Parents

1. What is ASD?

Autism spectrum disorder, or ASD, describes someone who has found something more interesting in life than socializing. Unfortunately, they have to live with social zealots, especially at school. With autism, the brain is wired differently. That means in certain areas such as mechanical, musical, mathematical, and drawing ability, there can be great talents, but often these may come at the cost of understanding people.

2. What Causes ASD?

As a follow-up question, parents often want to know what causes ASD. It is, at this stage, very difficult to determine just what's going on genetically. However, we clinicians may still say it is genetic. I believe this to be true in at least half the cases I see. As the Americans say, "The apple doesn't fall far from the tree." A parent could be an engineer, a specialist in information technology, a whiz in accountancy or medicine. These careers seem to be populated with a higher level of ASD than you'd expect. These are also careers that really embrace and benefit from the ASD thinking style. So for some, it may be that it is passed on through the family within and between generations.

For the others, it seems to be environmental. Now we don't know if it occurs in utero, perhaps by being exposed to toxic substances. We know certain prescriptions, such as an SSRI medication or an anti-convulsive medication, can be associated with ASD. It could also be in response to an infection, or it could be associated with unfavorable obstetric events. Finally, it may simply be a "one-off" event. Research continues.

3. What are the Chances of Having Another Child with ASD (aka Reoccurrence)?

Parents ask me, "I've got an ASD child; if we have another, what's the chance of ASD in that baby?" Current research suggests there's a one-in-three chance of recurrence, which is high. People need to be aware of that. Until the child is three or four, we can't say with certainty that they do or do not have ASD.

Another frequent question from parents is, "Why was it so rare years ago? Is it an epidemic?" I think there are more individuals being diagnosed with ASD today because we have greater accuracy in diagnoses. We've widened the goalposts to include ASD level one, formally known as Asperger's syndrome, and high-functioning autism. We also find that the number of kids diagnosed with mental retardation or intellectual disability has significantly dropped as ASD has increased. One can also have ASD as well as another disorder, such as Down's syndrome and autism, cerebral palsy and autism, blindness and autism; it is variable in its expression. With improved tools and insights, we are making better diagnoses.

That being said, with over forty-years' experience, I think there has been a marginal increase in the occurrence of ASD. The chances of having an ASD child increase when parents are age thirty-five and above. Today, people are delaying having children to establish their qualifications and career. They may be successful financially but obstetricians and gynecologists will advise you to have your kids young, not just because of fertility but also a risk of ASD. If I'm asked, "When should I start a family?" I say, "As soon as possible."

4. Can ASD Be Cured?

I never thought I would do this, but I am now starting to un-diagnose people. These are people who have generally had ASD features diagnosed early in life. There are some social skills that are intuitive and others that can be achieved by instruction. These people have taken programs on learning how to make friends, how to read faces, and they learned it! They've become sub-clinical in terms of testing below the ASD threshold.

I do think that there are some who can successfully dissolve most of the ASD diagnostic characteristics. They also tend to be those who do not have coexisting mood disorders, anxiety disorder, or depression. These conditions complicate social engagements, confidence, and self-esteem.

5. Child Management?

The fifth question category from parents is management of the child at home. It's critically important for both parents to align and practice the same management strategies. One parent cannot be a source of discipline or consequences while the other may understand more how ASD kids learn. Competing strategies

with ASD kids won't work. There's going to be resentment, revenge, and complications.

What works is understanding and explaining what the ASD child is supposed to do and encouraging and reinforcing that. Kids with ASD don't come with a manual. By definition, they're different. Conventional child-rearing strategies don't often work. Apply patience, optimism, and encouragement liberally.

Top Five Questions from Teachers

1. What Is the Best Learning Style?

Good teachers want their ASD kids to succeed. Their first question is usually, "What's the best learning style for someone with ASD?" Today, most classrooms are modeled in a social, conversational construct. This is the least effective way for those with ASD to learn. They learn best by looking at a computer or reading a book. In other words, by themselves. For some ASD students—the visualizers, engineers, and artists—a picture is worth a thousand words. So, basically, shut up and show them!

251

They learn by observation. There's another group that are verbal readers, they learn by reading texts on what to do.

One observation we've made of ASD students in a classroom setting is their problem with processing time. Classes filled with social interactions require thoughts of what to do next, and do not allow the ASD student intellectual capacity on the subject at hand. Sensory issues of noise, smells, touch, and confusion add to stress and anxiety. Thoughts become harder to process. As a result, overloads and meltdowns occur. These are the issues and constraints that we're very aware of.

We also find an association between ASD and learning disorders. ASD students can be hyperlexic or dyslexic, fantastic or hopeless with foreign languages, fluent with numbers of science, or they haven't a clue. Many are also natural artists as well as other extremes. With ASD, there is going to be very uneven profile of abilities. What I ask teachers to do is understand the ASD student's best learning style and make the curriculum Asperger's friendly.

2. Teamwork?

Schools and universities are increasingly expecting students to work in groups. With groupwork, you've added social dynamics which add distraction and confusion for an ASD student. As with a classroom setting, the kid with ASD is more concerned and overwhelmed with the social dynamics present rather than the group's task. I ask teachers or the group moderator, if possible, to commend the ASD student whenever they share, care, listen, help, cooperate, or join in. When you spot that he or she didn't read the social cue, assume that they didn't know what to do. At that point, I strongly recommend Carol Gray's *Social Stories*™ to teach the ASD student the appropriate action. At the adult level, it's successfully navigating teamwork that's going to determine whether he or she gets a job, so working on this skill is important.

3. Friendships?

You'll often find the ASD kid on the periphery of the playground, isolated from the others. They're exhausted from the mental processing needed in the classroom and they need solitude to drain their mind and calm down. Friendships, however, are a concern for them. They see the other kids playing and having fun and may even try to join in, but developmentally, they're often mentally younger, less physically gifted, and are perceived by others as more a liability than an asset. They need guidance and education in how to be a friend. That may mean bringing some kids who seem to understand him or her into the loop. This playground mentor should be encouraged to include the ASD person, to give them guidance and protection, and to look out for that child on the playground. Otherwise, the ASD child is going to come back into the classroom more exhausted than when they left.

4. Bullying and Teasing?

This discussion leads to another common question about bullying and teasing. The assumption is if they join in, they will meet friendly peers. But the predators will also find them and begin to exploit their weaknesses. For example, in ASD, if you're not good socially and you're not good at sports, the only thing you've got is your intellect, and you have a fear of making a mistake. Upon learning this vulnerability, a predator may say, "You're stupid. You don't know anything." They do it just to hurt. Kids with ASD can't understand why someone would want to hurt them intentionally. A teacher, a parent, or even the playground mentor (mentioned above) may have to explain to the ASD child what the predator is up to. But it may take more. Often, I tell teachers to look for other playground kids who are streetwise and popular to step in and stop it. That's the best way, a stronger peer saying, "This is zero-tolerance. We're a family here. It's not cool, it's not allowed. You leave him (or her) alone, because I'll report you to the teachers and this is serious." The ASD student must be protected from the predators.

5. How to Transition?

The fifth question often fielded from teachers is related to transitions. These transitions are between the various stages of elementary, junior high, and high school. Lots of preparation for a new school environment is necessary, because often the person with ASD finds the change difficult. Preparation for transition may involve visiting the new school, meeting new teachers, and settling in to the new environment, which can include after-school events. Successful navigation of these early transitions helps prepare the ASD student for college, the workforce, and life.

Bonus Sections

Top Five Questions from Public Servants

1. Employment Services?

Communities have a responsibility to employ people so they become taxpayers versus welfare recipients. The problem is, in the case of someone with ASD, not just any job will do. You've got to find the right job for the person; ASD has many talents.

If they find the right job, it's heaven! For the person with ASD, it's the best antidote to depression, it gives structure and purpose to the day, and it provides self-esteem and an income that one can spend on whatever they want. In Australia and parts of the United Kingdom, there are government agencies specifically designed to help those with Asperger's find a job. The US is only starting to advance in this area. However, the local autism associations, commonly found in larger US cities, often have job counselors and local programs to help ASD people find work.

Interestingly, with my colleagues Michelle Garnett and Jay Hobbs, we've now developed a curriculum called Thriving Now (see thrivingnow.net). It's a downloadable program to help those with ASD in their daily life, from the interpersonal skills needed in the job, when the job changes unexpectedly, sensory sensitivity, and the different way of learning new aspects of the job. Thriving Now is a program we've developed specifically to work in conjunction with agencies helping employment.

2. Emergency Medical Services?

A second question category comes from emergency health services professionals. Individuals with ASD can perceive the seriousness of discomfort or pain differently. At the scene of an accident, if a person with ASD is asked how they're feeling, the emergency medical technician may be asking for an intensity of the pain versus an understanding of the problem. Not truly sensing the pain or its implications, the person with ASD may say, "I'm fine. I'm okay," when in fact they may have a very serious medical issue. Education for the health services person is needed. Frontline health services professionals need to know the ASD profile. We also we need to train psychiatrists and psychologists in the nature of ASD, especially those in the areas of eating disorders, gender identity problems, alcohol and drug dependency services, and psychiatric hospitals. Pediatricians must also be educated in current ASD identification techniques. There's work to be done in this area.

3. Policemen, Firemen, Others?

"What do I do when I encounter someone with ASD?" As with emergency medical professionals, this is a common question from front line responders not experienced with ASD. If these people are policemen, firemen, or corrective services officers, it's especially important. Police may try and apprehend someone who doesn't necessarily follow instructions, who doesn't drop an instrument or weapon automatically, and appears in a disturbed state. They appear confused and overwhelmed, but most concerning, they don't obey the police officer. This can and has led to tragic consequences. It's important for police officers, corrective services, and firemen to a certain extent to understand the ASD profile and how to adjust accordingly. It needs to be a standard part of their training curriculum.

Regarding correction officers, this is especially important for me because my son William, who has Asperger's syndrome, spent two years in prison. He's currently writing and has just finished a manuscript on how to help people with Asperger's syndrome cope with being in prison. The circumstances were often horrendous for him. I hope his book will change people's understanding and attitudes in and outside the system.

4. The General Public?

The next area of public servants needing an education on ASD is the public itself. It's important for all of us to recognize that a neighbor or your child's friend at school may have the characteristics of ASD. The public needs to be informed about the values, eccentricities, gifts, and constraints of autism. It's a huge task, but as teachers and advocates, we all can make a difference. I do what I can through my practice, research, books, talks, articles, and interviews. I'm inspired daily by meeting Aspie mentors, parents, teachers, and others successfully educating the public, thereby advocating for our autism community.

5. The Church?

The final group of public servants asking to help is the church. Spiritual beliefs can be incredibly valuable for those with ASD. The church needs to understand the challenges these individuals face. The church can be very good in supplying a network of people to support the individual and their family, but it needs to be flexible with the social formality of the service. In a community setting, a response from someone with ASD to a piece of scripture might be unconventional; they may take the priest or pastor to task in terms of their own beliefs. But to someone loving someone on the spectrum, it's just part of the package. Patience on both sides goes a long way.

Ask Dr. Tony

Top Five Questions from Social Workers:

1. Family Stress Management?

Most people with loved ones on the spectrum have worked with the unsung heroes of social work. Often their questions are in recognition of the stress within the family of a child with ASD. The child can have intense emotions but sometimes parents find that the strategies of affection, consoling, compassion, and distraction just don't work. As a result, families or parents can be exhausted, confused, and overwhelmed. Social workers ask, "How can I help this family?" My answer to that is, "Listen." Sometimes they just need someone to explain, "This is ASD and it is not caused by bad parenting." That needs to be very clear from the social workers. They can say, "This is classic ASD, this has nothing to do with your competence as a parent. You're trying to do the best that you can." Parents need to know that.

2. Relationship Counseling?

A second question category is about the parent's relationship. One or both parents may have ASD characteristics that cause more friction. In an ASD/neurotypical pairing, the neurotypical may feel the person with Asperger's doesn't understand them. In counseling, the two will discuss the values and differences between ASD and NTs. Knowledge is power. This discussion can result in better understandings, value systems, and child-rearing strategies. Sometimes that needs to be dealt with by a relationship counselor. An astute social worker can spot this on the front line. They can help the family in so many ways!

3. Influence of an ASD Parent and Siblings?

The next question is often in relation to the siblings of the family with an ASD child. "Should a parent, brother, or sister have ASD, how's it going to affect the neurotypical children in that family?" I do workshops for neurotypical children who have an ASD parent.

Bonus Sections

I'll ask, "What's good about having an ASD parent?" One of the kids will say, "His knowledge of history is amazing! If I have a history essay or project to do, his knowledge is fantastic!" Then another kid might say, "I just want him to give me a simple answer. He gives me a one-hour lecture." I also get comments like, "Well, dad seems more in love with the dog and his computer than me." The other kids can feel sometimes that their brother or sister with ASD gets a disproportionate amount of their parent's time. They may feel left out or neglected. For social workers, it's important to recognize the challenges for neurotypical siblings. If available, alert the parents to possible neighborhood or group interactions for the siblings needing social opportunities outside the family.

4. Social Support for the Family?

As noted above, one role of the social worker is helping people reintegrate into society. Social workers have access to resources that provide support networks for the ASD family. This is incredibly important! As parents of ASD kids know, a wider distribution of support is necessary. Parents especially need time away to rest and recharge. For instance, social workers can help locate support groups for those who are a partner of someone with ASD. This is a wonderful opportunity for these neurotypicals to meet other NT partners and parents, and laugh and enjoy each other's stories with people who understand.

5. Navigating the System?

Paperwork is so confusing and consuming! As parents of ASD kids know, there are mountains of paperwork involved. Social workers help parents with the horrendous government forms needed to apply for all sorts of things. Since stressed parents are not experts in how governments work, these humble public servants often provide this support. Like so many unrecognized heroes in the autism community, I want to say to them, thank you for doing what you do!

CRAIG: A prevailing attitude throughout all these scenarios is that optimism helps. Always look for the good things!

DR. TONY: Exactly. If I could develop a pill for ASD, it would be a pill that gives you optimism. The Attwood family has a motto: "They can because they think they can!" That's optimism. And that's the attitude I encourage!

Author Craig Evans with one of his personal heroes, Dr. Tony Attwood

About the Authors

Craig R. Evans, MA, MBA

A former communications executive, Craig R. Evans is a film maker fascinated with traditional music, the banjo, and the community of players that celebrate this art form. His documentary series have been saved for posterity by Smithsonian Folkways.

Craig continues to be fascinated by people who think differently, especially his stepchild with Asperger's. Buoyed by daily gains toward independence and Dr. Attwood's boundless optimism, Craig promises to film, write, and speak encouraging news about autism as often as possible.

Ask Dr. Tony

Tony Attwood, PhD

Tony is a clinical psychologist who has specialized in autism spectrum disorders since he qualified as a clinical psychologist in England in 1975. He currently works in his own private practice, and is also adjunct professor at Griffith University, Queensland and senior consultant at the Minds and Hearts clinic in Brisbane. His book *Asperger's Syndrome: A Guide for Parents and Professionals* has sold over 400,000 copies and has been translated into twenty-seven languages. His subsequent book, *The Complete Guide to Asperger's Syndrome*, published in October 2006 has sold over 300,000 copies and has been translated into eighteen languages, and is one of the primary textbooks on Asperger's syndrome. He has several subsequent books published by Jessica Kingsley Publishers, Future Horizons Inc., and Guilford Press.

Tony has been invited to be a keynote speaker at many Australasian and International Conferences. He presents workshops and runs training courses for parents, professionals, and individuals with Asperger's syndrome all over the world and is a prolific author of scientific papers and books on the subject.

He has worked with many thousands of individuals of all ages with Asperger's syndrome or an autism spectrum disorder.

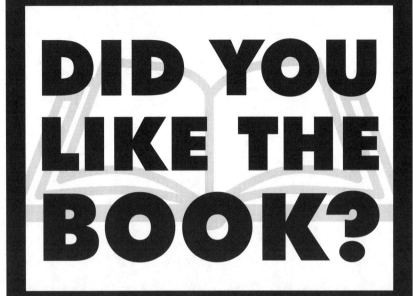